Turboprop Titan – The Global Story of Regional Aviation's Quiet Powerhouse

By

Aaron Aaberg

Copyright © 2025 by Aaron Aaberg

All rights reserved.

This edition published August 2025.

No part of this publication may be reproduced, stored in a retrieval system, or transmitted in any form or by any means—electronic, mechanical, photocopying, recording, or otherwise—without the prior written permission of the publisher, except for brief quotations used in reviews, academic work, or other non-commercial commentary, as permitted by applicable copyright law.

This work is protected by international intellectual property law. Any unauthorized use, reproduction, or distribution is strictly prohibited and may result in legal action.
Thank you for respecting the rights of the author and publisher.

"The measure of an aircraft is not how far it flies, but how many places it makes reachable."

Table of Contents

Foreword

Chapter 1: Foundations in Franco-Italian Partnership

Chapter 2: The First Step – ATR 42 Takes Flight

Chapter 3: Stretching the Concept – ATR 72 Emerges

Chapter 4: Beating the Odds – Competing with Jet Rivals

Chapter 5: Building a Global Footprint

Chapter 6: The U.S. Challenge

Chapter 7: Engineering Evolution – Upgrades and Enhancements

Chapter 8: Safety, Reliability, and Lessons Learned

Chapter 9: ATR and Environmental Efficiency

Chapter 10: Ownership Shifts and Airbus Involvement

Chapter 11: The Asian Ascendancy

Chapter 12: African Lifelines

Chapter 13: Latin America and the Caribbean Connection

Chapter 14: The Market for Second-Hand ATRs

Chapter 15: Freighter Conversions and Cargo Potential

Chapter 16: Inside the Cabin – Passenger Experience

Chapter 17: Manufacturing and Supply Chain

Chapter 18: Partnerships with Regional Airlines

Chapter 19: Competition and Consolidation

Chapter 20: The Next Generation – ATR 600 Series

Chapter 21: Short Runways and Remote Routes

Chapter 22: Training, Pilots, and Operations

Chapter 23: Economic Resilience and Market Survival

Chapter 24: ATR in the COVID-19 Era

Chapter 25: Hybrid Futures and Sustainable Aviation Fuel

Chapter 26: A Global Icon of Regional Aviation

Epilogue

Appendix A: Chronology of ATR Aircraft Development

Appendix B: Technical Specifications of Major ATR Variants

Appendix C: Global Operator List (Past and Present)

Foreword

In the grand sweep of aviation history, certain aircraft dominate the headlines, capture imaginations, and stand as symbols of technological ambition. The Concorde, with its supersonic allure, remains an icon of daring engineering. The Boeing 747, the "Queen of the Skies," came to embody mass international travel and globalization. And the Airbus A380, with its sheer size and complexity, has been celebrated as the pinnacle of widebody aviation. Yet alongside these headline-grabbing marvels exists another family of aircraft—quieter, more modest in their public profile, but no less essential to the way millions of people travel each year. They are the turboprops, and among them, no manufacturer has come to define the category more comprehensively than ATR.

For more than four decades, ATR has been at the heart of regional connectivity. Founded in the early 1980s as a Franco-Italian partnership between Aérospatiale of France and Aeritalia of Italy, ATR (Aerei da Trasporto Regionale/Avions de Transport Régional) built its reputation not on glamour but on reliability, accessibility, and efficiency. While widebody jets linked continents and high-speed trains revolutionized terrestrial transport in Europe and Asia, ATR carved out a unique role: connecting communities that would otherwise remain isolated. Its aircraft became the workhorses of short-haul travel, bridging islands, crossing mountain valleys, and landing on short, often challenging runways where larger jets could not venture.

The very geography of the world made ATR indispensable. In the scattered archipelagos of Indonesia and the Philippines, ATR aircraft became lifelines between hundreds of islands, delivering passengers, freight, and sometimes even medical supplies. In Africa, they connected secondary cities and remote regions, enabling economic development and mobility that jet services could never viably sustain. In Europe, ATRs slipped seamlessly into established aviation networks, linking regional hubs to major capitals, while in Latin America, they brought affordable, reliable service to mountainous areas and rural communities. From the Caribbean to the Canadian north, from South Asia to the Pacific islands, ATR has been present—quietly, consistently, and crucially.

The reason for this lies in the enduring value of the turboprop. While jets dazzled airlines and passengers with speed and prestige, turboprops offered an altogether different promise: unmatched fuel efficiency, lower operating costs, and performance ideally suited to sectors under 500 miles. For regional carriers, many of them operating on thin margins, these factors were decisive. Turboprops burn significantly less fuel than jets on short-haul routes, making them both economically and environmentally advantageous. As fuel prices fluctuated and environmental concerns grew, the humble turboprop revealed itself as not a relic of the past but a prescient tool for the future.

ATR understood this dynamic better than most. From the moment the ATR 42 first entered service in 1985, the company pursued a clear mission: to dominate the regional turboprop market through incremental refinement, adaptability, and close alignment with airline needs. The strategy was remarkably successful. By the early 1990s, ATR had expanded its product line with the larger ATR 72, which quickly became its best-selling model. Together, the ATR 42 and 72 came to define regional aviation, with thousands of units delivered across six continents.

What makes ATR particularly remarkable is not just its market share, but its longevity. Aviation is a notoriously volatile industry, where companies rise quickly and often fall just as fast. Regional aircraft in particular have seen many manufacturers emerge with promise only to disappear in the face of competition or economic downturns. Names like Fokker, Saab, and Fairchild once represented strong regional brands but ultimately faded. ATR, by contrast, endured. It adapted to changes in ownership, technological shifts, and evolving airline economics, all while maintaining its singular focus on turboprops. Even as rival Bombardier wound down its Dash 8 program in the 2010s, ATR continued to thrive, positioning itself as the last major turboprop manufacturer standing.

This book seeks to tell the story of how ATR achieved that status—not with the spectacle of revolutionary breakthroughs, but through steady progress, pragmatic decisions, and the ability to stay relevant in a shifting aviation landscape. It is a story of industrial collaboration across national borders, of careful attention to market niches, and of a commitment to building aircraft that, above all else, do the job reliably. It is also a story of how a relatively quiet company managed to influence global mobility in ways that are often invisible to the casual observer but deeply felt by the communities it serves.

To understand ATR's significance, one must appreciate what short-haul air travel means in practice. For millions of passengers each year, it is not about luxury or speed but about necessity. A farmer in rural Indonesia, a doctor traveling between Caribbean islands, a businessperson connecting from a provincial town to a major city—these are the passengers ATR was built to serve. The turboprop is not the aircraft of long-haul glamour, but of everyday life. It is the bridge between the global and the local, the enabler of opportunity, and the guarantor of connectivity where other forms of transport cannot reach.

The chapters that follow trace this journey in full: from ATR's founding in the early 1980s, through its battles with jet rivals, its expansion into every corner of the globe, its technical evolution, its challenges, and its resilience. Along the way, we will examine not only the aircraft themselves, but also the people and airlines that made them successful, the industrial framework that kept them in production, and the economic and environmental arguments that ensure their continued relevance.

In many ways, ATR embodies a paradox. It is one of the most important aircraft manufacturers in the world, yet its name rarely appears in mainstream conversation outside of industry circles. Its products have carried hundreds of millions of passengers, yet few travelers could identify the type of aircraft they were flying on. It is an empire not of prestige but of presence—an empire built on quiet success, measured not in headlines but in steady, reliable service.

As aviation looks ahead to new challenges—sustainability, hybrid-electric propulsion, and shifting travel patterns in a post-pandemic world—ATR once again finds itself in a position of quiet importance. The same qualities that made turboprops indispensable in the 1980s—efficiency, adaptability, and suitability for short-haul travel—now align with the demands of a greener, more resource-conscious age. If the past four decades have proven anything, it is that ATR's role is not a fleeting chapter but a continuing narrative in the story of aviation.

This is the history of ATR: not a story of glamour, but of persistence; not of spectacle, but of substance. It is the story of how a company dedicated to the humble turboprop became one of aviation's most enduring and quietly influential empires.

Chapter 1: Foundations in Franco-Italian Partnership

The late 1970s and early 1980s marked a period of profound change for the aviation industry. On one end of the spectrum, the widebody revolution was in full swing, with aircraft like the Boeing 747, the Lockheed L-1011 TriStar, and the McDonnell Douglas DC-10 redefining long-haul travel. On the other, regional and commuter aviation was undergoing its own transformation. Smaller propeller-driven aircraft, once the preserve of local operators and lightly regulated markets, were becoming increasingly important as national governments deregulated air travel and airlines sought to expand networks into smaller cities and less-developed regions. Yet the available fleet of regional aircraft was fragmented, dominated by aging designs or small manufacturers with limited reach. It was in this environment that France and Italy—two nations with long histories in aerospace—saw the opportunity to create something new, pooling resources and industrial know-how to establish a strong European presence in the regional market. The result was ATR.

The roots of ATR lie in the recognition that no single European country could, by itself, compete effectively against American aerospace giants. By the early 1980s, the United States had already established itself as the dominant force in regional aircraft production, with names like Fairchild, Beechcraft, and De Havilland (whose Dash 8 program, although Canadian, was heavily linked to the North American market). European nations, however, had a wealth of aeronautical expertise spread across multiple firms but lacked the scale to challenge transatlantic competitors individually. The emergence of Airbus in the 1970s, itself a pan-European effort, demonstrated that cooperation across national borders could yield not only technologically advanced products but also globally competitive companies. France's Aérospatiale and Italy's Aeritalia took this lesson to heart.

Aérospatiale, formed in 1970 from the merger of several French aerospace companies, was already a key player in both civil and military aviation. Its portfolio included helicopters, missiles, and participation in Airbus, as well as the Concorde supersonic airliner. Aeritalia, established in 1969 as a consolidation of Italy's aerospace industry, brought its own strengths in military transport aircraft and aerostructures. Both companies were searching for opportunities to expand in the civil aircraft sector beyond their existing commitments. The regional market presented itself as a logical arena: it was less capital-intensive than building large jets, yet growing rapidly thanks to airline liberalization and rising demand for short-haul travel.

The idea of a joint regional turboprop was first floated in the late 1970s, when both Aérospatiale and Aeritalia were independently studying potential commuter aircraft designs. Rather than pursue separate projects that risked competing with one another and dividing already limited resources, the companies began discussions about collaboration. The political context favored such cooperation. Both France and Italy were committed members of the European Economic Community, and governments were eager to encourage industrial projects that demonstrated the benefits of continental integration. Aerospace was an especially potent symbol of this, combining cutting-edge technology with strategic importance. A joint Franco-Italian aircraft program would not only strengthen Europe's position in civil aviation but also reinforce political ties at a moment when Europe was striving to assert greater industrial autonomy.

The economic rationale was equally compelling. The regional aircraft market was forecast to expand significantly in the 1980s, driven by airlines seeking to serve thinner routes that could not sustain jet operations. These routes demanded aircraft with seating capacities of around 30 to 70 passengers, optimized for short sectors under 500 miles. Turboprops were ideally suited for this environment: they offered lower fuel consumption than jets at these distances, could operate from shorter runways, and required less ground infrastructure. For smaller carriers or regional subsidiaries of larger airlines, such characteristics were vital. Yet the options available to them were limited. Many still relied on piston-engine aircraft or early-generation turboprops like the Fokker F27, which, though reliable, were increasingly outdated. Newer designs were emerging, but the market remained fragmented. This created a gap that Aérospatiale and Aeritalia believed they could fill with a modern, efficient turboprop.

In 1981, the partnership was formally launched under the name ATR—Aerei da Trasporto Regionale in Italian, Avions de Transport Régional in French. The bilingual designation symbolized the balance between the two partners, while also emphasizing the shared European identity of the project. The new company would not manufacture aircraft entirely independently; instead, it would serve as a joint venture responsible for design, development, and marketing, with production work shared between the French and Italian parent firms. This arrangement mirrored the model established by Airbus, which had demonstrated that multinational cooperation could be structured in a way that distributed both costs and benefits across borders.

The division of labor between Aérospatiale and Aeritalia was carefully negotiated. Aérospatiale took responsibility for the forward fuselage, cockpit, and systems integration, while Aeritalia contributed the wings and rear fuselage. Final assembly would take place in Toulouse, France, leveraging the city's growing status as a hub of European aerospace activity thanks to Airbus. This structure ensured that both nations retained significant industrial involvement while avoiding duplication of effort. It also made political sense, as both governments could point to tangible economic and employment benefits from the partnership.

From the outset, ATR was conceived not as a single-aircraft program but as a family of regional turboprops. The initial focus was on a 40–50 seat model, which became the ATR 42. This size was chosen deliberately, positioned between smaller commuter aircraft and larger regional jets, giving it flexibility to serve both niche routes and higher-density short-haul sectors. The decision to start with a mid-sized design reflected a broader strategic calculation: by offering an aircraft that could appeal to a wide range of airlines, ATR hoped to build a customer base that would sustain future expansions of the product line.

The collaboration also reflected a broader European ambition to assert independence from American technological dominance. In the 1960s and 1970s, Europe had often played catch-up in commercial aviation, but projects like Airbus showed that when European nations worked together, they could produce world-class aircraft. ATR was a smaller-scale version of this vision. While it did not seek to compete with the giants of long-haul travel, it represented a determination to ensure that Europe remained competitive across the full spectrum of aviation markets.

Of course, cooperation between two companies from different countries was not without its challenges. Cultural differences, organizational structures, and differing design philosophies had to be reconciled. Engineers from Aérospatiale and Aeritalia worked closely together, often navigating not only technical but also linguistic and procedural differences. Decision-making required compromise, and there were moments of tension as each side sought to ensure its interests were represented. Yet both partners were united by the recognition that the success of the program depended on presenting a cohesive product to the market. Fragmentation would only undermine the effort.

One of the earliest challenges was choosing the engine. Turboprop engines were critical to performance, efficiency, and reliability, and the wrong choice could doom the aircraft before it even reached customers. After evaluating several options, ATR selected the Pratt & Whitney Canada PW120 series, a new generation of turboprop engines that offered excellent fuel efficiency and reliability. The decision to use a Canadian engine underscored ATR's pragmatism: although the project was European, it was willing to source the best available technology globally to ensure competitiveness. This willingness to blend European design with international components would become a hallmark of ATR's strategy.

As development work progressed, the broader aviation market reinforced the logic of ATR's creation. Deregulation in the United States, launched in 1978, was spurring a boom in regional airlines and commuter services, creating a surge in demand for economical short-haul aircraft. Europe, though still heavily regulated, was beginning to show similar trends, with regional carriers seeking to expand connectivity beyond the traditional major hubs. In Asia, Africa, and Latin America, economic growth was creating new opportunities for air travel in markets ill-suited to large jets. ATR was positioned to meet these diverse needs with a single family of aircraft adaptable to different conditions.

When the ATR 42 was unveiled in 1984, the response from airlines confirmed that the Franco-Italian gamble had been well placed. Orders began to flow in from regional operators who saw the aircraft as a modern alternative to older turboprops. The program validated the notion that cross-border European cooperation could succeed not only in the glamorous world of widebody jets but also in the quieter yet equally vital domain of regional aviation.

The establishment of ATR also had symbolic significance beyond the aviation industry. It embodied a growing

European confidence that collaboration was not just desirable but necessary to compete globally. In the decades that followed, ATR would continue to expand, evolve, and adapt, but its foundation in the early 1980s was the crucial moment that set it on its path to becoming the world's leading regional turboprop manufacturer.

The Franco-Italian partnership that created ATR was, in essence, a blend of pragmatism and vision. Pragmatism, because both Aérospatiale and Aeritalia recognized that alone they lacked the resources to build a globally competitive regional aircraft. Vision, because together they foresaw the enduring importance of short-haul connectivity and the role turboprops could play in sustaining it. Their decision to join forces not only launched a successful company but also helped shape the very structure of regional air travel for decades to come.

As the ATR 42 prepared for its maiden flight, the partnership's true test was only just beginning. Building the company and designing the aircraft were significant achievements, but the real measure of success would lie in whether ATR could convince airlines worldwide that its turboprops were the future of regional travel. The Franco-Italian foundations were strong; now they needed to carry the weight of global expectations.

Chapter 2: The First Step – ATR 42 Takes Flight

When the ATR 42 made its first flight on August 16, 1984, it marked more than just the rollout of another regional aircraft. It symbolized the culmination of several years of Franco-Italian industrial collaboration and the entry of a new contender into a market that was about to undergo dramatic transformation. The aircraft's debut in the skies above Toulouse was both a technical milestone and a political statement, proof that Europe's aerospace industry could create a competitive product in a segment that had long been dominated by American and Canadian manufacturers. The journey from paper concept to airborne reality was shaped by technical decisions, market forecasts, and the pressing need to deliver an aircraft that could balance performance, efficiency, and reliability.

The ATR 42 was born into a competitive environment. By the early 1980s, the regional airliner market was seeing renewed vitality. Deregulation in the United States had unleashed a flood of new commuter airlines that needed modern aircraft. In Europe, although regulatory structures remained tighter, regional carriers were beginning to expand services beyond national borders, especially as the European Economic Community encouraged greater integration. At the same time, older turboprops such as the Fokker F27, the Handley Page Herald, and the Hawker Siddeley 748 were approaching obsolescence. Their piston-era roots and limited efficiency made them less appealing to operators struggling with rising fuel prices. Bombardier's de Havilland Canada Dash 8, launched in 1983, represented the most direct competition for ATR. The Dash 8 offered modern avionics and good short-field performance, but it was initially produced in smaller sizes, seating around 37 passengers. ATR saw its opportunity to offer a slightly larger aircraft, optimized for 42 seats, that would meet airline needs for low operating costs on short-haul routes.

From the beginning, the design philosophy of the ATR 42 emphasized efficiency. The chosen Pratt & Whitney Canada PW120 turboprop engines provided the power needed for short-field performance while consuming less fuel than comparable jet engines. With its high-mounted wings, the ATR 42 offered excellent lift and stability, crucial for operations into airports with challenging approach paths or less-than-ideal runway conditions. The aircraft's landing gear, mounted on stub wings extending from the fuselage, allowed for a cabin floor closer to the ground, easing boarding and cargo handling without the need for elaborate ground infrastructure. These features were not just conveniences; they were essential to airlines operating in regions where airports lacked modern facilities.

Certification was another major hurdle, and ATR needed to satisfy both European and American regulators if it hoped to sell globally. European certification was handled by the French Directorate General for Civil Aviation (DGAC), while the U.S. Federal Aviation Administration (FAA) also scrutinized the design. The ATR 42 achieved its European certification in September 1985, followed by FAA certification soon after. This dual approval underscored the seriousness of the project and ensured that the aircraft could be marketed worldwide. Certification processes examined not only the aircraft's performance but also its safety, systems reliability, and compliance with international standards. For a new manufacturer like ATR, successfully navigating this process was itself a validation of its technical competence.

The first customer deliveries in 1985 went to French regional airline Air Littoral, which put the ATR 42 into service on routes along the Mediterranean coast. Almost immediately, the aircraft proved its worth. Airlines appreciated its fuel economy and the straightforwardness of its systems. Passenger feedback was generally positive, noting the comfortable cabin and relatively quiet engines compared to older turboprops. The cabin layout allowed for up to 50 passengers in a 2-2 seating configuration, with a cabin width comparable to many jets in service at the time. While not luxurious, it provided a level of comfort that matched the expectations of regional travelers.

One of the key selling points of the ATR 42 was its low operating cost per seat mile. Airlines in the 1980s were grappling with volatile fuel prices, and the turboprop's efficiency made a decisive difference in profitability. On routes under 300 miles, where jet speeds offered little advantage, the ATR 42 outperformed regional jets in economic terms. The aircraft's simple systems also contributed to lower maintenance costs, further endearing it to operators with limited technical resources. In many respects, the ATR 42 represented exactly the kind of aircraft airlines were seeking: not flashy, but practical and reliable.

The early success of the ATR 42 helped secure orders from a variety of airlines across Europe and beyond. Regional carriers in France, Italy, and Spain adopted the type, but the aircraft also found customers in North America, Asia, and Africa. Its ability to handle diverse operating environments—short runways, hot and high conditions, and limited infrastructure—made it attractive to operators in developing countries. In Latin America, for example, the ATR 42 quickly became popular with airlines serving mountainous regions and remote communities. In the Caribbean, its ability to hop between islands on short legs made it a natural choice.

As production ramped up in the mid-1980s, ATR's Toulouse facility became the center of a new industrial rhythm. Components from Aeritalia's factories in Italy arrived for final assembly in France, embodying the cross-border cooperation that defined the project. The sight of Italian-built wings being married to French fuselages in Toulouse symbolized not just an aircraft coming together, but also a European vision of industrial integration. The ATR 42's rollout into service was accompanied by aggressive marketing, with ATR emphasizing the aircraft's cost savings and adaptability.

Despite its successes, the ATR 42 faced challenges. Competing against the Dash 8 was a constant reality, as Bombardier sought to expand its own market share with successive versions of its turboprop. Some airlines were hesitant to commit to a brand-new manufacturer, preferring the established pedigree of companies like de Havilland or Fokker. Moreover, the rise of regional jets in the late 1980s presented a looming threat. Aircraft such as the BAe 146 and

Embraer's early jets promised speed and passenger appeal, even if they could not match the operating economics of turboprops. ATR had to work hard to convince airlines that the 42-seat turboprop still had a long-term future.

What ATR had on its side was timing. The ATR 42 entered the market just as global airlines were searching for exactly the kind of efficiency it offered. Fuel efficiency was more important than speed on many short routes, and the aircraft's relatively low purchase price made it appealing to smaller carriers. Its performance characteristics also made it more versatile than many jets: it could access airports that were off-limits to jets due to short runways or noise restrictions. This versatility became one of the ATR 42's defining strengths, opening doors to markets that competitors could not easily serve.

The aircraft's design also allowed for incremental improvements, which ATR introduced through successive sub-variants. The ATR 42-300, the original production version, was followed by the ATR 42-320 with more powerful engines for better hot-and-high performance. The ATR 42-500, introduced later in the 1990s, featured upgraded avionics, improved noise reduction, and greater passenger comfort. These enhancements demonstrated ATR's commitment to evolving the platform to meet customer needs, a strategy that would serve the company well throughout its history.

The ATR 42's role in shaping regional airlines cannot be overstated. For many operators, acquiring ATR 42s allowed them to expand networks, open new routes, and compete more effectively. In some cases, the aircraft enabled airlines to operate scheduled services where previously only charter or irregular flights had been possible. In developing countries, ATR 42s often became the backbone of domestic fleets, connecting remote communities to national capitals and fostering economic development.

By the end of the 1980s, ATR had secured a strong foothold in the regional market. The ATR 42 had not only proven itself as a viable aircraft but also established the company's reputation as a serious manufacturer. With more than 200 orders placed within the first few years of production, ATR had demonstrated that its Franco-Italian partnership could produce a globally competitive product. The ATR 42's early success laid the foundation for future growth, giving ATR the confidence to expand its product line and challenge rivals on an even larger scale.

The impact of the ATR 42 was also symbolic. For Europe, it showed that industrial cooperation across borders could deliver results not just in the high-profile world of widebody jets but also in the quieter, less glamorous but equally vital regional segment. The aircraft represented a European answer to the challenges of short-haul aviation, one that combined technical competence with market pragmatism. For airlines and passengers, it offered a new level of reliability and efficiency, reshaping expectations of what a regional aircraft could deliver.

The launch of the ATR 42 was, in every sense, a first step. It validated the idea of ATR as a viable manufacturer, provided airlines with a modern turboprop solution, and set the stage for the company's expansion with larger aircraft. The challenges of competition, evolving market dynamics, and technological change would continue, but the ATR 42 had secured its place in aviation history as the aircraft that introduced the world to ATR and launched what would become the most successful turboprop program in history.

The success of the ATR 42 also brought with it a new question: could the formula be scaled up? Airlines increasingly demanded greater capacity as passenger volumes grew, and many of the very routes where ATR 42s were thriving were now beginning to justify larger aircraft. ATR's response would be to stretch its concept, applying the same design philosophy to a new model with more seats and improved economics. That evolution would come to life in the form of the ATR 72, unveiled before the decade was out.

Chapter 3: Stretching the Concept – ATR 72 Emerges

The success of the ATR 42 during its first years of operation gave the Franco-Italian partnership a solid foundation in the competitive regional aviation market. By the mid-1980s, ATR had proven that its collaborative model could produce a commercially viable and technically competent turboprop. Yet, the very strengths that had made the ATR 42 a success also revealed its limitations. Airlines quickly recognized the aircraft's efficiency and reliability, but in many markets, demand was outpacing the aircraft's capacity. The next logical step for ATR was to offer something larger—an aircraft that retained the proven design philosophy of the ATR 42 but provided more seats, better economics for higher-demand routes, and expanded appeal to airlines seeking fleet commonality with increased capacity. This was the genesis of the ATR 72.

The decision to create a stretched version of the ATR 42 was shaped by both market forces and competitive pressures. By the mid-1980s, the regional airline industry was undergoing rapid expansion, especially in Europe and Asia. Deregulation in the United States had shown the potential of regional carriers, but in Europe, liberalization was unfolding more gradually. Still, demand for short-haul connectivity was growing, and larger regional aircraft were increasingly in demand. Competitors were already moving in this direction. Bombardier's Dash 8 program had begun to evolve, and Fairchild Dornier and Fokker were considering or developing larger regional aircraft. If ATR wanted to remain competitive and expand its market reach, it needed to offer an aircraft that could carry more passengers while maintaining the low operating costs that defined the ATR 42.

In 1985, only a year after the ATR 42's first flight, ATR formally launched the ATR 72 program. The aircraft would be a stretched derivative of the 42, sharing most of its systems, engines, and design features but lengthened to accommodate up to 74 passengers. This stretch was significant, representing nearly a 75 percent increase in capacity compared to the 42-seat baseline. The new aircraft would allow airlines to increase frequencies or reduce costs per seat by carrying more passengers per flight. Importantly, ATR designed the 72 to share a high degree of commonality with the 42. This meant that airlines operating both types would benefit from simplified pilot training, maintenance procedures, and spare parts inventories. For regional carriers with tight budgets and limited resources, this was a powerful selling point.

Technically, the ATR 72 retained the ATR 42's high-mounted wing and twin-engine turboprop configuration. The fuselage was lengthened by 4.5 meters (approximately 15 feet), creating space for additional rows of seats. To support the increased weight and higher capacity, ATR upgraded the landing gear and made structural reinforcements throughout the airframe. The wingspan was slightly increased, and more powerful versions of the Pratt & Whitney Canada PW100 series engines were installed. These improvements allowed the ATR 72 to maintain the short takeoff and landing capabilities that had made the ATR 42 so versatile, even with the larger airframe.

From a performance standpoint, the ATR 72 was designed to deliver the same efficiency advantages as its smaller sibling but at greater scale. On routes with sufficient passenger demand, the economics of the larger aircraft were even more compelling. Airlines could carry more passengers without a proportional increase in fuel burn, reducing unit costs and improving profitability. This was especially important in regions where airports imposed slot restrictions or where demand justified higher-capacity flights without sacrificing frequency.

The ATR 72 made its first flight on October 27, 1988, just four years after the ATR 42's maiden flight. Certification was achieved in 1989, and the aircraft entered service soon after with Finnair as one of the launch customers. The timing of the ATR 72's introduction proved fortunate. Airlines were increasingly under pressure to contain costs while meeting growing passenger demand, and the ATR 72 offered an ideal balance of capacity, efficiency, and operational flexibility.

Passenger experience in the ATR 72 was broadly similar to the ATR 42, with a 2-2 seating layout that allowed for a relatively spacious cabin compared to many commuter aircraft of earlier generations. The aircraft could be configured to seat between 64 and 74 passengers, depending on airline preference. Larger overhead bins, improved soundproofing, and incremental cabin upgrades made the aircraft more appealing to travelers. While it lacked the speed of jets, the ATR 72 offered a comfortable and economical alternative for short-haul flights, particularly where journey times were under an hour.

The first years of ATR 72 service confirmed the wisdom of ATR's decision to stretch its concept. Orders flowed in from airlines across Europe, Asia, and Latin America. Regional carriers in France, Spain, and Italy adopted the type, while international operators in markets as diverse as Thailand, Brazil, and the Philippines quickly added it to their fleets. The aircraft's ability to operate into secondary airports with short or narrow runways was a decisive factor. In many countries, ATR 72s became the default choice for regional airlines expanding connectivity to smaller cities or linking islands and remote regions.

One of the most significant features of the ATR 72 was its fleet commonality with the ATR 42. Airlines could operate both types interchangeably on routes of different demand levels, optimizing capacity without incurring the costs of operating two completely distinct aircraft families. Pilots trained on the ATR 42 could transition to the ATR 72 with minimal additional instruction, reducing training costs and increasing crew flexibility. Maintenance crews, likewise, could service both types with the same tools and procedures. This level of commonality was highly attractive to regional operators, many of whom had limited budgets and infrastructure.

ATR also took care to ensure that the ATR 72 evolved through successive variants, incorporating feedback from airlines and technological improvements. The initial ATR 72-100 was followed by the ATR 72-200, which offered improved performance and higher takeoff weights. Later, the ATR 72-210 introduced even more powerful engines, providing better performance in hot-and-high conditions. By the mid-

1990s, the ATR 72-500 had emerged, featuring upgraded avionics, improved passenger comfort, and noise reduction systems. This commitment to incremental improvement reinforced ATR's reputation as a manufacturer attuned to its customers' needs.

The ATR 72's popularity was particularly strong in regions with geographic constraints. In the Philippines, Cebu Pacific and Philippine Airlines relied heavily on ATR turboprops to connect the archipelago's more than 7,000 islands. In Indonesia, airlines such as Merpati and later Lion Air and Wings Air built extensive domestic networks using ATR 72s. In Europe, airlines like Air Dolomiti, Alitalia, and Olympic Airways deployed ATR 72s on short routes where jets were impractical. In Latin America, carriers in Colombia, Brazil, and the Caribbean used the ATR 72 to serve regional airports inaccessible to larger aircraft. The aircraft's presence in Africa was equally important, with airlines like Air Botswana, Precision Air, and Royal Air Maroc relying on ATRs to provide vital domestic and regional connectivity.

Despite its success, the ATR 72 was not without challenges. Competition from Bombardier's Dash 8 series was constant, particularly as Bombardier introduced larger versions such as the Dash 8-300 and later the Dash 8-400 (also known as the Q400). These aircraft offered higher speeds and, in the case of the Q400, significantly greater performance. However, ATR countered by emphasizing its aircraft's superior economics on short sectors. While the Dash 8 could fly faster, the ATR 72 consumed less fuel, making it more cost-effective on routes under 300 miles. For many regional airlines, cost efficiency mattered more than speed, and this gave ATR a crucial advantage.

Another challenge came from the growing popularity of regional jets in the 1990s. Aircraft like the Embraer ERJ-145 and the Bombardier CRJ series offered jet speed and passenger appeal, leading some airlines to phase out turboprops in favor of jets. In markets like the United States, where consumer perception strongly favored jets, this trend was particularly pronounced. However, ATR managed to maintain a strong position by focusing on markets where turboprops were indispensable. In countries with shorter runways, limited infrastructure, or fragmented geography, regional jets could not compete effectively. ATR's strategy was not to challenge jets directly, but to dominate the segment where turboprops were the only viable option.

The ATR 72's impact extended beyond airline economics to broader questions of accessibility and connectivity. In many parts of the world, the aircraft enabled new routes that had never before been possible with larger aircraft. This had profound social and economic consequences. Communities in remote regions gained access to reliable air transport, improving access to markets, healthcare, and education. Tourism boomed in regions where ATR 72s connected secondary destinations to international gateways. For governments seeking to promote regional development, ATR aircraft became critical infrastructure assets.

By the mid-1990s, ATR had delivered hundreds of ATR 72s, and the type was firmly established as the leading regional turboprop in its class. The company's dual-family strategy—

offering both the ATR 42 and 72—gave it flexibility to serve different markets while maximizing customer loyalty. Airlines that started with ATR 42s often upgraded to ATR 72s as their markets matured, creating a natural progression path. ATR's ability to keep both aircraft families competitive through continuous improvement ensured that customers remained invested in the brand.

The ATR 72's success also reinforced the value of the Franco-Italian partnership. By building on the foundations of the ATR 42 and extending the concept into a larger aircraft, ATR demonstrated that it could innovate while preserving its core strengths. The project validated the idea that European industrial cooperation could succeed not only in theory but in practice, producing aircraft that were commercially successful on a global scale.

Looking back, the introduction of the ATR 72 was more than just a product launch. It represented a critical evolution in ATR's strategy, allowing the company to expand its market share and solidify its position as the world's leading turboprop manufacturer. It also demonstrated the foresight of ATR's leadership in recognizing that the regional market was not static but dynamic, requiring continuous adaptation to meet evolving airline needs.

For passengers, the ATR 72 became a familiar sight around the world, from the islands of the Pacific to the rural airstrips of Africa, from bustling European regional airports to Latin American mountain towns. It was not glamorous, but it was dependable. Its quiet, efficient service became the backbone of countless regional networks, and its presence in airline fleets shaped the way millions of people traveled.

As ATR entered the 1990s, the ATR 72 gave the company confidence to face new challenges. Regional jets were rising, competition was intensifying, and the global economy was shifting. Yet, the ATR 72 ensured that ATR was not merely surviving but thriving. By stretching the concept of the ATR 42, the company had created a versatile, efficient, and globally relevant aircraft that would continue to define short-haul aviation for decades to come.

Chapter 4: Beating the Odds – Competing with Jet Rivals

By the early 1990s, ATR found itself at a crossroads. The ATR 42 and ATR 72 had established the Franco-Italian manufacturer as a serious player in the regional aviation market. Deliveries were healthy, and the aircraft were proving their worth on routes across Europe, Asia, Africa, and Latin America. Yet even as ATR celebrated its early success, a new and potentially existential challenge was taking shape: the rapid rise of regional jets. These sleek aircraft, often marketed as the modern face of regional travel, threatened to eclipse turboprops by appealing to both airlines and passengers with their speed, comfort, and perceived modernity. For ATR, the 1990s would be defined not only by the expansion of its product line but also by its ability to convince airlines—and the traveling public—that turboprops still had a vital role to play in short-haul aviation.

The appeal of jets was easy to understand. Throughout the history of aviation, jets had symbolized progress and modernity. Passengers associated jet travel with speed, comfort, and prestige, while propeller-driven aircraft were often seen as outdated or second-best. By the late 1980s, regional jets were becoming increasingly available, offering airlines the opportunity to upgrade their image and attract customers who preferred the idea of flying in a jet. Manufacturers such as Bombardier with its Canadair Regional Jet (CRJ) series and Embraer with the ERJ family were pushing aggressively into the regional market. Even British Aerospace offered the BAe 146 "Whisperjet," a four-engine regional jet designed for short-haul operations into noise-sensitive airports. For many airlines, these new jets seemed like the future.

The challenge for ATR was that turboprops could not match jets for speed. On routes over 300 miles, jets had a clear advantage in journey time. They also offered smoother ride quality at higher altitudes, another factor that appealed to passengers. Airlines looking to upgrade their brand image often favored jets because they believed it would help them compete more effectively against mainline carriers. Turboprops, by contrast, were often relegated to short feeder routes, and in some markets, passengers viewed them as noisy, bumpy, and less comfortable. This perception problem was perhaps ATR's greatest hurdle.

But while jets had their strengths, ATR knew that turboprops retained distinct advantages—advantages that were particularly compelling in the operational and economic realities of regional aviation. The most important of these was fuel efficiency. Turboprops consumed significantly less fuel than jets on short sectors under 300 miles. This difference was not marginal; it could amount to 30–40 percent less fuel burn per flight, a decisive factor at a time when airlines were struggling with volatile fuel prices. Lower fuel consumption translated into lower operating costs, which meant that turboprops could make routes profitable that would be uneconomical for jets.

The second advantage was infrastructure compatibility. Turboprops like the ATR 42 and 72 could operate from shorter runways than regional jets, giving them access to hundreds of airports around the world that jets could not use.

This was particularly important in regions with limited infrastructure, such as island nations, mountainous areas, or developing countries. In Indonesia, the Philippines, the Caribbean, and much of Africa, ATR aircraft became the only practical solution for scheduled air service. Jets, for all their appeal, were simply not capable of serving these markets.

Another key advantage was acquisition and maintenance cost. Turboprops were less expensive to purchase than jets, making them more accessible to small regional carriers. Their systems were simpler, and their engines generally required less costly maintenance than jet engines. For airlines operating on thin margins, this made turboprops more sustainable. ATR also emphasized the commonality between the ATR 42 and 72, which allowed operators to benefit from reduced training and spare parts costs. In contrast, airlines purchasing regional jets often had to invest heavily in new training programs, infrastructure, and support equipment.

ATR recognized that its survival depended on more than just touting the economics of turboprops. The company had to actively reshape the narrative around its aircraft, positioning them not as relics of the past but as practical, modern solutions for the realities of regional travel. Marketing campaigns highlighted the efficiency and versatility of ATR aircraft, focusing on the ability to connect communities that jets could not reach. ATR also worked closely with airlines to demonstrate the profitability of turboprop operations, providing detailed analyses showing how their aircraft could make marginal routes viable.

Passenger perception remained a challenge, but ATR and its airline partners invested in improving the turboprop experience. Cabin noise reduction systems, better soundproofing, and more comfortable seating layouts helped counter the stereotype of turboprops as noisy and cramped. The ATR 72-500, introduced in the 1990s, featured significant improvements in passenger comfort, including quieter engines, new interiors, and modern avionics. These upgrades helped ATR convince airlines that turboprops could offer a passenger experience comparable to jets on short-haul routes.

Despite the rise of jets, ATR found strong allies among regional airlines that prioritized economics over image. Carriers in Europe, such as Air Littoral, Air Dolomiti, and Olympic Airways, relied heavily on ATRs for their short-haul networks. In Asia, airlines like Bangkok Airways and Mandarin Airlines expanded their fleets with ATR 72s to serve regional destinations. In Africa, where runway conditions and infrastructure were often limited, ATRs became indispensable. Even in Latin America, where competition from jets was fierce, ATR carved out a niche by serving secondary cities and challenging airports.

The 1990s also saw the emergence of low-cost carriers, a trend that played to ATR's strengths. Airlines seeking to minimize costs and maximize efficiency often turned to ATR turboprops as the backbone of their regional fleets. For example, carriers in the Caribbean and Southeast Asia built business models around high-frequency, low-cost flights using ATRs. The aircraft's ability to operate multiple short sectors in a single day with low fuel consumption made them ideal for this emerging model of air travel.

At the same time, ATR had to contend with the aggressive expansion of its primary competitor, Bombardier. The Dash 8 series, particularly the larger -300 and -400 variants, offered strong performance and higher speeds than ATR's turboprops. Bombardier marketed these aircraft as a middle ground between turboprops and jets, appealing to airlines that wanted turboprop efficiency with closer-to-jet performance. The Dash 8-400, introduced in the late 1990s, could carry up to 78 passengers at speeds approaching those of regional jets. For ATR, this was a formidable challenge.

Yet even in the face of this competition, ATR maintained its position by focusing relentlessly on the economics of short-haul operations. Independent analyses consistently showed that the ATR 72 burned less fuel than the Dash 8-400 on flights under 300 miles. While the Dash 8 was faster, the difference in flight time was often less than 10–15 minutes, a margin that mattered little to passengers on short regional flights. Airlines operating ATRs could therefore offer lower fares or higher profitability, a decisive advantage in the price-sensitive regional market.

ATR also benefited from strategic backing by its parent companies. Aérospatiale and Aeritalia (later Alenia Aeronautica) ensured that ATR had the industrial resources and political support needed to weather competitive pressures. Airbus's growing influence, as Aérospatiale merged into the larger European aerospace consortium, further strengthened ATR's global reach by providing access to marketing networks and customer support infrastructure. These connections helped ATR maintain visibility and credibility in a crowded market.

Throughout the 1990s, the battle between turboprops and regional jets played out across global markets. In North America, jets increasingly dominated, as consumer preference for jet travel was particularly strong and fuel prices were relatively low. Many U.S. regional carriers phased out turboprops in favor of CRJs and ERJs, relegating ATR to a smaller role. But in Europe, Asia, Africa, and Latin America, ATR held its ground and even expanded. The company's ability to adapt its sales strategies to different markets was critical. Where passenger perception favored jets, ATR emphasized the economics of secondary routes and niche markets. Where infrastructure limited jet operations, ATR positioned itself as the only viable option.

The company's resilience during this period was remarkable. Many predicted that turboprops would fade into obsolescence in the face of jets, yet ATR not only survived but thrived. Its strategy of incremental improvement, combined with a relentless focus on cost efficiency, ensured that it retained a loyal customer base. By the end of the decade, ATR had delivered more than 500 aircraft, a testament to its ability to compete effectively even in a challenging market.

The broader context of the 1990s also worked in ATR's favor. Rising fuel prices in the latter half of the decade reminded airlines of the value of fuel efficiency. Environmental concerns, though still nascent, began to shape aviation policy in Europe, creating new arguments for turboprops. Governments in developing countries invested in regional connectivity, often relying on ATR aircraft to provide essential services. All of these factors reinforced ATR's relevance at a time when jets seemed poised to dominate.

Perhaps the most telling measure of ATR's success in competing with jets was the way in which its aircraft became embedded in the global aviation landscape. By the late 1990s, it was almost impossible to travel in many parts of the world without encountering an ATR. From Caribbean island-hopping services to domestic routes in Thailand, from rural connections in France to inter-island flights in Indonesia, ATR turboprops were everywhere. They were not glamorous, but they were indispensable.

The 1990s thus established ATR's identity as the champion of turboprops in a jet-dominated era. The company proved that efficiency, versatility, and reliability could beat speed and prestige in the markets that mattered most. By doing so, ATR not only secured its survival but also laid the groundwork for future growth. The competition with jets was far from over, but ATR had shown that turboprops could beat the odds and carve out a lasting place in global aviation.

Chapter 5: Building a Global Footprint

By the dawn of the 1990s, ATR had firmly established itself as a viable manufacturer of regional turboprop aircraft. With the ATR 42 proving its worth and the ATR 72 gaining traction, the Franco-Italian partnership had demonstrated that Europe could create and sustain a successful regional airliner program. Yet, survival in aviation required more than technical achievement or early success. To thrive, ATR needed to establish a truly global presence, embedding itself into the airline networks of every continent and becoming indispensable in markets far beyond Europe. The decade that followed would see ATR do exactly that, expanding its customer base and weaving its aircraft into the fabric of regional connectivity around the world.

The key to ATR's global expansion was the universal nature of the problem it sought to solve. Every region of the world had cities, towns, and islands that could not support jet operations but still required reliable air service. In some cases, geography made air travel essential: islands scattered across the Caribbean or the Pacific could only be connected by air. In others, mountainous terrain made road or rail travel impractical, while airports built decades earlier lacked the runway length or infrastructure needed for jets. These conditions created natural markets for turboprops. ATR recognized this early and pursued a sales strategy that highlighted the aircraft's adaptability to diverse environments.

Europe remained ATR's home market and a critical base of operations. Regional airlines such as Air Littoral in France,

Air Dolomiti in Italy, and Olympic Airways in Greece were early adopters of the ATR family, using the aircraft to link smaller cities with major hubs. In Scandinavia, airlines such as Finnair and Widerøe employed ATRs to serve remote communities across Finland and Norway, where short runways and harsh weather challenged other aircraft types. The ability of ATRs to operate safely and reliably in these conditions strengthened their reputation as rugged and dependable. The European Union's gradual liberalization of air travel in the 1990s further encouraged the growth of regional airlines, creating more opportunities for ATRs to expand.

Asia-Pacific quickly emerged as one of ATR's strongest growth regions. The geography of countries such as Indonesia and the Philippines, composed of thousands of islands, made turboprops not just useful but essential. In Indonesia, Merpati Nusantara Airlines, Garuda Indonesia's domestic arm, and later Wings Air built extensive regional networks with ATRs. The aircraft provided lifeline services, carrying passengers, cargo, and mail between islands that lacked reliable ferry or road connections. In the Philippines, both Philippine Airlines and Cebu Pacific integrated ATRs into their fleets, with Cebu Pacific eventually becoming one of ATR's largest operators worldwide. The aircraft's ability to operate from short runways and basic airstrips made it indispensable in these markets, where many airports were little more than paved strips in remote locations.

Thailand offered another example of ATR's penetration into Asia. Bangkok Airways, branding itself as "Asia's Boutique

Airline," built much of its early network around ATR aircraft. The airline's operations to secondary Thai cities and tourist destinations such as Koh Samui and Sukhothai relied on the ATR 72, which could land on shorter runways and offered the efficiency needed for short domestic hops. Mandarin Airlines in Taiwan, along with operators in India, Malaysia, and Vietnam, further expanded ATR's footprint across the region. By the late 1990s, Asia had become a core market for ATR, with the aircraft serving as the backbone of regional connectivity across multiple countries.

Africa represented another natural market for ATR, one that highlighted the aircraft's ability to operate in challenging conditions. Many African nations had large, sparsely populated territories with limited ground infrastructure. Roads were often poor, and rail networks limited, making air travel the only practical means of connecting remote communities. However, many airports across the continent featured short, rough runways, making jets unsuitable. ATR aircraft proved ideal for this environment. Airlines such as Air Botswana, Air Mauritius, and Precision Air in Tanzania adopted ATRs, using them to connect rural areas with national capitals and international gateways. Royal Air Maroc also employed ATRs for domestic and regional services, while carriers in countries like Nigeria, Cameroon, and Madagascar followed suit. ATRs became lifelines, transporting not only passengers but also medical supplies, food, and essential goods. In many African nations, the arrival of ATR aircraft meant that air travel was no longer limited to elites but became accessible to broader sections of the population.

Latin America and the Caribbean offered yet another fertile market for ATR. The region's geography, with mountainous terrain in the Andes and archipelagos in the Caribbean, created strong demand for short-haul aircraft. In Colombia, Avianca and SAM Colombia used ATRs to serve secondary cities and regional airports nestled in valleys and mountainous areas. Brazil, with its vast distances and regional diversity, also saw significant ATR adoption, particularly by regional airlines that later became integrated into larger carriers. In Mexico, Aeromar relied heavily on ATR turboprops to connect smaller cities and tourist destinations, operating them across the country's challenging topography. In the Caribbean, airlines such as LIAT (Leeward Islands Air Transport) and Caribbean Star Airlines depended on ATRs to hop between islands, often operating multiple sectors per day on short routes. The rugged reliability of the ATR made it especially suited to these high-frequency operations.

The North American market proved more difficult for ATR, reflecting cultural and economic dynamics distinct from other regions. In the United States, the deregulated environment of the 1980s had spurred growth in regional airlines, but by the 1990s, consumer preference had tilted strongly toward jets. Many U.S. passengers viewed turboprops as noisy and outdated, preferring regional jets like the Bombardier CRJ or Embraer ERJ. Nevertheless, ATR found some footholds. American Eagle, the regional affiliate of American Airlines, operated ATR 42s and ATR 72s extensively during the 1990s, particularly from its hubs in Dallas/Fort Worth and Miami. The aircraft served routes to smaller cities in Texas, the southern United States, and the Caribbean. Continental Express also employed ATRs in its fleet, while other U.S. regional carriers adopted the aircraft in smaller numbers. However, as regional jets became more widespread in North America, ATR's presence gradually diminished. Still, its aircraft remained common in Mexico and Canada, where economics and geography favored turboprops for certain routes.

While geographic conditions drove much of ATR's global expansion, strategic sales and marketing also played crucial roles. ATR worked tirelessly to demonstrate to airlines the economic benefits of its aircraft, often providing detailed performance comparisons that highlighted lower fuel burn, reduced operating costs, and greater profitability on short-haul routes. The company emphasized the commonality between the ATR 42 and 72, stressing how airlines could operate both types seamlessly, adjusting capacity to match demand. This strategy proved particularly effective for small and medium-sized carriers that needed flexibility without the burden of maintaining multiple aircraft families.

Another factor in ATR's global success was the strength of its customer support network. Recognizing that many of its customers operated in remote or developing regions with limited technical resources, ATR invested heavily in training, maintenance support, and spare parts logistics. Training centers were established in Toulouse and Miami, with additional facilities later opened in Asia and other regions. These centers provided simulator training for pilots, maintenance instruction for engineers, and operational support for airlines. ATR's emphasis on customer support helped cement long-term relationships with airlines, ensuring that operators felt confident in their ability to maintain and operate the aircraft efficiently.

ATR also understood the importance of adapting to the specific needs of different markets. For example, in hot-and-high environments such as Latin America and parts of Africa, airlines required aircraft with enhanced engine performance. ATR responded with upgraded versions of the ATR 42 and 72, incorporating more powerful engines and increased takeoff weights. In other regions, airlines valued quietness and passenger comfort, leading to improvements in noise insulation and cabin layouts. By tailoring its product development to customer feedback, ATR built a reputation as a responsive manufacturer attuned to the realities of regional operations.

By the end of the 1990s, ATR had firmly established itself as a global player. Its aircraft were in service with more than 100 airlines across six continents, operating in some of the most diverse and challenging environments on earth. The ATR 42 and 72 had become the default choice for regional connectivity in many countries, their versatility and efficiency proving decisive against both older turboprops and newer regional jets. Importantly, ATR had managed to not only survive but thrive in an industry where many competitors had faltered. Manufacturers such as Fokker, Saab, and British Aerospace saw their regional programs struggle or disappear, while ATR continued to grow.

The global footprint that ATR built during this period had long-lasting consequences. In Asia, Africa, and Latin America, ATRs became so deeply embedded in airline fleets and national transport systems that replacing them with other types would have been difficult. The aircraft became part of the identity of regional carriers, with their distinctive silhouettes recognizable at airports from Colombo to Pointe-à-Pitre, from San José to Nairobi. In many communities, the arrival of an ATR represented not just a flight but a connection to the wider world.

For ATR, building a global footprint was not simply about selling aircraft; it was about embedding itself into the infrastructure of aviation worldwide. By aligning its product with the needs of regional carriers, investing in customer support, and continuously refining its designs, ATR secured its place as the world's leading turboprop manufacturer. The quiet empire it was building was not measured in flashy marketing campaigns or the glamour of long-haul jets but in the steady hum of turboprop engines connecting communities that might otherwise remain isolated.

As the new millennium approached, ATR stood at the threshold of another era of challenges and opportunities. The company had proven its global relevance, but competition from Bombardier's Dash 8 and the continuing rise of regional jets meant that it could not rest on its achievements. The next phase of its journey would require not just maintaining its global footprint but defending and expanding it in the face of shifting economic, technological, and environmental dynamics.

Chapter 6: The U.S. Challenge

For all its global reach, ATR faced one of its greatest hurdles in the United States, the world's largest aviation market. Success in Europe, Asia, Africa, and Latin America had demonstrated the versatility and resilience of its aircraft, but North America proved to be a stubborn and often hostile environment. The reasons were complex: a mixture of regulatory restrictions, passenger perceptions, competition from domestic manufacturers, and the peculiarities of U.S. regional airline dynamics. While ATR did find customers in the United States, its fortunes were mixed at best, and its experience there highlights the challenges of bringing a European turboprop into a market that was often predisposed against it.

The American commuter and regional airline sector had been reshaped dramatically by deregulation in 1978. With the Airline Deregulation Act, carriers gained the freedom to choose routes and set fares without government oversight, leading to an explosion of new airlines and services. Major airlines responded by developing hub-and-spoke networks, relying on regional partners to feed traffic into their hubs from smaller communities. This new ecosystem created demand for a new generation of regional aircraft—larger and more capable than the piston twins and small turboprops that had previously dominated, but smaller and cheaper to operate than the mainline jets. It was in this context that ATR sought to gain a foothold.

On paper, the ATR 42 and 72 were ideally suited to the U.S. regional market. They offered the right capacity, operating economics, and performance to serve the short-haul feeder routes that proliferated after deregulation. Yet, several factors conspired against ATR. The first was competition from domestic and Canadian manufacturers. American carriers, often under political and economic pressure to "buy American," favored aircraft built by companies such as Fairchild and de Havilland Canada, whose Dash 8 was heavily marketed in the United States after Bombardier's acquisition. The Dash 8 gained an early edge with U.S. carriers thanks to its combination of good performance, local support, and the perception of being a more "domestic" product.

ATR's biggest break in the U.S. came through American Eagle, the regional affiliate of American Airlines. In the late 1980s and early 1990s, American Eagle became one of ATR's largest operators, integrating both ATR 42s and ATR 72s into its fleet. From its bases at Dallas/Fort Worth and Miami, American Eagle operated ATRs extensively, serving smaller cities in Texas, the Southeast, and the Caribbean. The aircraft were particularly well suited to routes in Florida and the Caribbean, where short sectors and airport limitations played to the turboprop's strengths. For several years, ATRs became a common sight in American Eagle's livery, giving the European manufacturer a level of visibility in the United States that it might otherwise have struggled to achieve.

Continental Express was another important U.S. customer. The regional subsidiary of Continental Airlines employed ATR 42s and ATR 72s on routes from Houston and Newark, again serving smaller cities and thinner routes that could not sustain jets. These contracts gave ATR credibility in the American market, showing that its aircraft could integrate into the U.S. regional system. Other carriers, such as Trans World Express and Simmons Airlines, also operated ATRs in smaller numbers.

Despite these successes, ATR faced significant obstacles. Passenger perception was perhaps the most difficult to overcome. In the United States, where jet travel had long been associated with progress and modernity, turboprops carried an image problem. Many passengers viewed them as noisy, slow, and outdated, preferring the idea of boarding a sleek jet. Regional jets, which began to enter the market in the early 1990s, only heightened this perception. The Bombardier CRJ and Embraer ERJ families offered jet speed and jet prestige at a regional scale, and airlines quickly embraced them as a way to upgrade their image. Passengers often voted with their feet, choosing airlines that offered jets on regional routes over those that still operated turboprops. This cultural bias toward jets was stronger in the United States than in almost any other market, and it proved a major handicap for ATR.

Regulatory factors added to the difficulties. In the early 1990s, ATR encountered a major challenge in the form of U.S. Federal Aviation Administration (FAA) scrutiny over its aircraft's performance in icing conditions. In 1994, an American Eagle ATR 72 crashed near Roselawn, Indiana, while on approach in freezing rain, killing all 68 people on board. The National Transportation Safety Board (NTSB) investigation found that the aircraft had suffered from severe icing beyond its certification envelope, leading to a loss of control. The accident was a devastating blow to ATR's reputation in the United States. Although the investigation ultimately pointed to a combination of rare weather conditions and inadequate pilot training as key factors, the image of ATR aircraft as being vulnerable in icing conditions lingered. The FAA imposed restrictions on ATR operations in certain weather conditions, and airlines reassessed their use of the aircraft.

The Roselawn accident underscored the differences between operating environments in Europe and the United States. While icing conditions exist worldwide, the severity and frequency of certain types of freezing rain in North America posed unique challenges. ATR responded by working with regulators and operators to enhance de-icing systems, improve pilot training, and clarify operating procedures. Over time, the restrictions were adjusted, and ATR's aircraft were recognized as safe within their certified limits. Nevertheless, the damage to passenger and airline perception was significant, and ATR's U.S. presence never fully recovered from the incident.

Meanwhile, regional jets were rapidly gaining ground. Airlines like Comair, SkyWest, and Atlantic Southeast Airlines embraced the Bombardier CRJ and Embraer ERJ families, marketing them aggressively as modern, fast, and comfortable alternatives to turboprops. The economics of regional jets were less favorable on short sectors, but U.S. airlines often prioritized image and passenger preference over raw efficiency. For major carriers, upgrading their feeder services to jets also helped them compete more effectively with rivals, as passengers increasingly expected jet service even on short routes. This trend accelerated through the 1990s and 2000s, pushing turboprops to the margins of the U.S. market.

The contrast with other regions of the world was stark. While ATR thrived in Asia, Africa, and Latin America, where turboprops were indispensable, in the United States they were increasingly seen as second-class. Even airlines that had once been strong ATR customers began to retire the type in favor of jets. American Eagle gradually phased out its ATR fleet in the 2000s, replacing them with regional jets. Continental Express followed a similar path, and other carriers reduced their turboprop operations. By the mid-2000s, ATR's footprint in the United States had shrunk dramatically, leaving only a handful of operators in niche markets.

Yet, ATR's story in the United States was not one of outright failure. For nearly two decades, ATR aircraft played a significant role in American regional aviation, particularly in the South, Midwest, and Caribbean. Thousands of passengers flew on ATRs each day, often without realizing they were on a European aircraft. For airlines, the ATR provided an economical solution during a transitional period in regional aviation. Even after their retirement from major carriers, many ATRs continued to find second lives with smaller operators, cargo carriers, or international airlines.

One area where ATR did find a lasting role in the United States was cargo. The ATR 42 and 72 proved well suited to regional freight operations, particularly in feeder networks for major cargo airlines. FedEx Express became a major operator of ATR freighters, using converted aircraft to connect smaller markets to its hubs in Memphis and Indianapolis. The aircraft's efficiency and ability to operate from short runways made them ideal for cargo operations into secondary airports. Even as passenger airlines moved away from ATRs, the freighter market kept the type flying in the United States.

ATR's mixed fortunes in the U.S. reflect the unique characteristics of the American aviation landscape. Cultural preference for jets, fierce competition from domestic manufacturers, and regulatory challenges created an environment in which turboprops struggled to thrive. Yet, the ATR's presence, particularly in the fleets of American Eagle and Continental Express, demonstrated that its aircraft could play a significant role even in this difficult market. The lessons ATR learned in the United States—about passenger perception, regulatory compliance, and competition with jets—would shape its strategies in other regions for decades to come.

By the early 2010s, ATR's role in the U.S. passenger market had largely ended, but its aircraft continued to serve in cargo operations and with a few niche passenger carriers. Globally, ATR's fortunes remained strong, proving that while the United States was a challenging market, it was not the only one that mattered. Indeed, the contrast between ATR's struggles in the U.S. and its success elsewhere highlighted the diversity of global aviation. In much of the world, turboprops were not only relevant but essential. In the U.S., they were marginalized—but even there, ATR left a legacy that endured through its aircraft's continued service in freight and regional niches.

ATR's American challenge demonstrated the resilience of the company. Despite setbacks, including high-profile accidents and cultural biases against turboprops, ATR continued to innovate and expand globally. The U.S. experience was a reminder that success in aviation is never universal, but that adaptability, persistence, and focus on core strengths can carry a manufacturer through even the most difficult markets. For ATR, the mixed fortunes in the United States became part of the larger story of how a European turboprop manufacturer built a global empire—quietly, persistently, and with an understanding that not every market could be won, but that enough could be to ensure enduring success.

Chapter 7: Engineering Evolution – Upgrades and Enhancements

One of the defining characteristics of ATR's success has been its ability to refine and evolve its aircraft steadily over the decades rather than attempting to reinvent them with radical changes. In an industry where major redesigns are expensive, risky, and often subject to long delays, ATR adopted a philosophy of incremental improvement. This approach allowed the company to keep its aircraft competitive against rivals, respond to airline feedback, and ensure long-term market relevance. The ATR 42 and 72 that entered service in the mid-1980s bore the hallmarks of this philosophy from the beginning, but it was in the years that followed that ATR demonstrated how continual upgrades and enhancements could sustain a program for decades.

The foundation of this evolutionary strategy was the ATR 42-300, the original production version certified in 1985. Powered by two Pratt & Whitney Canada PW120 engines, it was a capable and efficient turboprop, but like all new aircraft, it reflected the design and technology of its era. Airlines operating in hot-and-high conditions quickly identified the need for more power, while operators in noise-sensitive environments sought quieter engines. ATR responded by introducing the ATR 42-320, featuring more powerful PW121 engines and incremental improvements in performance. This responsiveness to customer needs established a pattern that ATR would follow consistently: rather than waiting for a complete new design cycle, the company introduced upgrades in response to real-world operations.

The same philosophy applied to the ATR 72, which entered service in 1989. The initial ATR 72-100 gave airlines the higher capacity they needed, but ATR soon began introducing improvements with the ATR 72-200. This variant featured higher maximum takeoff weights and stronger performance, enabling operations in more demanding environments. ATR continued the process with the ATR 72-210, also known as the "hot and high" version, equipped with even more powerful engines to handle airports at altitude or in hot climates. Each of these incremental improvements reflected the company's awareness that the global nature of its customer base demanded flexibility. What worked for an airline in Northern Europe might not work for a carrier in the Andes or sub-Saharan Africa, and ATR's ability to tailor its aircraft to these conditions was a major advantage.

By the 1990s, airlines were increasingly focused not only on performance but also on passenger comfort and noise reduction. The public perception of turboprops as noisy and less comfortable than jets was a barrier to their acceptance in certain markets. ATR addressed this head-on with the ATR 42-500 and ATR 72-500, which represented major steps forward in cabin comfort and systems modernization. Introduced in the mid-1990s, the -500 series featured six-bladed propellers, which reduced noise and vibration significantly compared to earlier four-bladed designs. Cabin interiors were upgraded with better soundproofing, improved lighting, and more comfortable seating. From a passenger perspective, the changes were noticeable: ATR cabins became quieter, smoother, and more pleasant, narrowing the comfort gap with regional jets.

The -500 series also introduced avionics upgrades, with modernized flight decks that simplified pilot workload and improved safety. Glass cockpit technology, which was becoming standard in larger aircraft, was incorporated into ATR designs, giving crews digital displays that provided more information and reduced reliance on traditional analog gauges. These enhancements not only improved operational safety but also made ATR aircraft more appealing to airlines, which could reduce training costs by aligning with the avionics philosophies of larger fleets.

Fuel efficiency remained a constant focus of ATR's engineering evolution. The PW127 engines, used on later ATR variants, provided not only greater power but also improved fuel burn characteristics. Combined with aerodynamic refinements, these upgrades kept ATR's operating costs consistently lower than those of competing turboprops and regional jets. Airlines evaluating short-haul routes often found that ATR aircraft remained the most economical option, even decades after the original designs had entered service. This was no small achievement in an industry where technological obsolescence can come quickly.

Beyond engines and avionics, ATR made continuous improvements in weight reduction, materials, and systems integration. Structural enhancements allowed for higher payloads and greater durability, while refinements in maintenance procedures reduced downtime and operating costs. ATR invested in making its aircraft easier to maintain, with modular systems that simplified component replacement. For airlines in remote regions, where spare parts and technical expertise might be scarce, these improvements were critical. The ability to keep aircraft flying reliably with minimal infrastructure was a selling point ATR emphasized in its marketing and support programs.

One of ATR's most significant milestones came with the introduction of the ATR -600 series in 2009. This represented the most comprehensive upgrade in the program's history, building on decades of incremental evolution. The -600 series featured new avionics, new interiors, and improved engines, effectively bringing the aircraft up to 21st-century standards without requiring an all-new design. The cockpit was equipped with a new Thales glass cockpit, with five LCD screens, a modern autopilot system, and improved communication and navigation capabilities. These upgrades aligned ATR's cockpit technology with that of contemporary Airbus aircraft, simplifying training and making the aircraft more appealing to airlines that operated mixed fleets.

The cabin of the -600 series was also redesigned with a focus on passenger experience. Larger overhead bins, more spacious interiors, LED lighting, and modern design elements created a more comfortable and attractive environment. ATR branded this cabin "Armonia," highlighting its emphasis on harmony between comfort and efficiency. By investing in passenger experience, ATR directly addressed one of the longstanding criticisms of turboprops and helped reposition them as competitive with jets in terms of comfort.

Performance improvements in the -600 series were equally important. New Pratt & Whitney PW127M engines provided more power, better fuel efficiency, and reduced emissions. The aircraft's takeoff and landing performance was further enhanced, allowing it to operate into even shorter runways and more challenging airports. These capabilities reinforced ATR's reputation as the most versatile regional turboprop, able to access markets that were beyond the reach of jets or less efficient competitors.

Importantly, ATR's evolutionary approach kept costs manageable for both the manufacturer and its customers. Developing an all-new aircraft design can cost billions of dollars, a prohibitive investment for a niche manufacturer. By contrast, ATR's strategy of continuous improvement allowed it to maintain competitiveness with far lower development costs. Airlines also benefited, as upgrades often came in the form of improved variants that could be integrated into existing fleets with minimal disruption. The continuity of design meant that pilot training, maintenance practices, and spare parts inventories remained consistent across generations, reducing lifecycle costs.

Another area of engineering evolution was cargo capability. As global e-commerce expanded in the 2000s and 2010s, demand for regional freighters grew. ATR responded with factory-built freighter versions of the ATR 42 and 72, as well as conversion programs for passenger aircraft. These freighter variants featured large cargo doors, reinforced floors, and optimized interiors for cargo handling. The ATR 72-600F, introduced in 2017, was the first purpose-built regional freighter in decades, offering airlines and logistics companies an efficient solution for short-haul cargo operations. This diversification into cargo extended the lifecycle of ATR's designs and opened new revenue streams.

Environmental performance also became a major focus of ATR's enhancements. The company highlighted the lower CO_2 emissions of turboprops compared to regional jets, positioning its aircraft as environmentally responsible choices in an industry under increasing scrutiny for its carbon footprint. Engineering improvements in engines, aerodynamics, and weight reduction contributed to further emissions reductions, aligning ATR with the growing emphasis on sustainability in aviation. Later, ATR invested in certification for sustainable aviation fuels (SAF) and began research into hybrid-electric propulsion, ensuring that its evolutionary philosophy extended into the realm of future technologies.

ATR's ability to sustain its aircraft families through continual upgrades also gave it a competitive advantage over rivals. Bombardier's Dash 8 program, while successful, faced higher costs and complexity, particularly with the introduction of the Dash 8-400. Other competitors, such as Saab and Fokker, exited the regional aircraft market entirely, leaving ATR as the sole major manufacturer of turboprops by the 2010s. This was not the result of a single technological breakthrough but rather of steady, deliberate engineering evolution. By making the right upgrades at the right time,

ATR kept its products relevant, reliable, and attractive to airlines long after their initial introduction.

The story of ATR's engineering evolution underscores the importance of listening to customers and adapting to changing conditions. Each enhancement—from more powerful engines to quieter cabins, from improved avionics to freighter conversions—was driven by specific airline needs and market trends. ATR's engineers focused not on dramatic reinvention but on practical improvements that delivered tangible benefits. The result was a product line that remained competitive for more than three decades, an extraordinary achievement in an industry where aircraft programs often struggle to remain viable for even half that time.

Today, the ATR 42 and 72 stand as testaments to the power of incremental innovation. The aircraft that entered service in the 1980s has been transformed through successive upgrades into a thoroughly modern platform, capable of meeting the demands of 21st-century aviation. Passengers boarding an ATR 72-600 may not realize that they are flying on an aircraft whose basic design dates back to the 1980s, so thoroughly have the upgrades modernized the experience. For airlines, the continuity of design combined with continual improvement has delivered unmatched efficiency and value.

ATR's strategy of engineering evolution has not only ensured its survival but also cemented its dominance in the turboprop sector. While competitors disappeared or shifted focus, ATR remained steadfast, proving that sometimes the quiet path of incremental progress can be the most effective. The lessons learned from this approach would serve the company well as it faced future challenges in safety, environmental performance, and market dynamics, ensuring that the ATR story was not one of fleeting success but of enduring relevance.

Chapter 8: Safety, Reliability, and Lessons Learned

The success of any aircraft manufacturer does not rest solely on efficiency, comfort, or market reach. In aviation, safety and reliability are the ultimate measures of credibility. For ATR, a company whose aircraft often operate in some of the world's most challenging environments, from short island hops to mountainous regions with limited infrastructure, safety has been an unavoidable test of endurance. Over its decades of service, ATR has faced scrutiny, investigations, and operational lessons from accidents and incidents. Its ability to respond, adapt, and improve has been central not only to its reputation but also to its survival in an industry where a single misstep can jeopardize confidence among airlines and passengers alike.

When the ATR 42 entered service in 1985, it was designed with the modern standards of safety mandated by European regulators of the time. The aircraft's systems included redundancies typical of commercial aviation, such as dual hydraulic circuits, multiple flight control backups, and reliable Pratt & Whitney Canada turboprop engines. As with any new aircraft program, however, it would be real-world operations that revealed areas where additional improvements could be made. The ATR 42's introduction was generally smooth, but as its global fleet grew into the hundreds, and later thousands with the ATR 72, the manufacturer inevitably encountered the realities of operating in diverse climates, under varied levels of pilot training, and in airports that ranged from world-class hubs to rough strips carved into remote landscapes.

The 1990s became the period in which ATR faced some of its most severe challenges to its safety reputation. The ATR 72, in particular, was involved in a pair of high-profile accidents in icing conditions that would forever shape how ATR aircraft—and indeed all turboprops—were viewed in relation to winter operations. In October 1994, American Eagle Flight 4184, an ATR 72-212 operating between Indianapolis and Chicago, crashed after encountering severe icing while holding near Roselawn, Indiana. The aircraft experienced an uncommanded roll and loss of control, killing all 68 people on board. Investigators determined that ice accretion on the wings beyond the de-icing boots contributed to a phenomenon known as "ice bridging," where ice builds up aft of protected surfaces, altering aerodynamic properties.

The Roselawn accident had profound consequences. The U.S. Federal Aviation Administration (FAA) issued directives grounding ATR aircraft until modifications could be made, and airlines began to question whether turboprops were adequately prepared for the most severe icing environments. ATR, together with Pratt & Whitney Canada and regulators, responded by developing modifications to de-icing systems, improving operating procedures for crews, and enhancing training for icing scenarios. These changes included extending the span of de-icing boots, altering airspeeds in icing conditions, and revising pilot checklists. The incident underscored that turboprops, which often operated at altitudes where icing was more frequent than at the higher cruise levels of jets, required robust protection against freezing conditions.

Tragically, icing issues surfaced again in 1997, when another ATR 72, operating as Comair Flight 3272 near Detroit, crashed in similar winter conditions. This accident reinforced the urgent need for comprehensive solutions, not only in aircraft design but also in operational standards. ATR responded with further technical modifications, and regulators imposed stricter certification requirements for turboprops operating in icing-prone areas. The lessons learned from these events shaped ATR's approach for decades, ensuring that safety in icing conditions remained a top engineering and operational priority. By the 2000s, the company could demonstrate that the changes had been effective, as ATR aircraft continued to operate successfully in North America, northern Europe, and other regions with severe winters.

Beyond icing, ATR faced other challenges that revealed the importance of reliability and operational resilience. In 1987, an ATR 42 operated by Continental Express crashed on approach to Houston after encountering wind shear, emphasizing the vulnerability of smaller aircraft in sudden weather phenomena. While wind shear was not unique to ATR, the incident highlighted the need for enhanced crew training and better weather radar systems. In response, ATR integrated improved avionics and weather radar into its aircraft, aligning with broader industry advancements.

Mechanical reliability was another critical dimension of ATR's evolution. From the outset, the Pratt & Whitney Canada engines chosen for the ATR 42 and 72 were known for their durability, but maintaining consistent reliability across global operations required ongoing improvements. Airlines operating in dusty, hot environments—such as parts of Africa or India—reported challenges with engine wear. ATR and its suppliers responded with adaptations to improve filtration and maintenance schedules. Similarly, airlines flying on short sectors with frequent takeoffs and landings needed assurance that cycles of pressurization and power changes would not compromise safety. ATR established rigorous maintenance programs, ensuring that its aircraft maintained strong reliability metrics, often exceeding industry averages for dispatch reliability.

The human factor also played a role in ATR's safety narrative. As regional airlines expanded rapidly in the 1980s and 1990s, pilot training varied widely across operators. While major carriers had robust training programs, some smaller airlines in emerging markets lacked the same resources. This occasionally led to incidents where improper procedures, rather than design flaws, contributed to accidents. ATR worked closely with airlines and regulators to strengthen training standards. Simulator programs were expanded, operational documentation was refined, and ATR created partnerships with training organizations to ensure that crews flying its aircraft were adequately prepared.

Public perception is another dimension of safety. Accidents, even if rare in statistical terms, can disproportionately shape how the public views a particular aircraft. After the Roselawn crash in the United States, ATR turboprops developed an unfair reputation among some passengers as less safe in winter conditions, despite technical improvements and rigorous oversight. ATR engaged in outreach, emphasizing data showing that its aircraft met the highest safety standards. Over time, as reliability improved and incidents declined, confidence in the ATR returned, particularly outside the U.S., where airlines continued to operate the aircraft extensively in diverse conditions.

Reliability also extended beyond safety into operational dependability. Airlines valued ATR aircraft not only because they were economical but also because they could be trusted to perform day after day. By the 2000s, ATR was boasting dispatch reliability rates of over 99 percent, meaning that delays due to mechanical issues were rare. This placed ATR on par with, or ahead of, many jet competitors, dispelling any perception that turboprops were less dependable. Airlines operating thin-margin regional routes depended on this reliability, as even minor disruptions could have outsized financial impacts.

The evolution of ATR's safety and reliability story also reflected broader trends in aviation. Each incident or challenge provided lessons that shaped not only ATR but also industry standards. For example, the icing accidents of the 1990s spurred industry-wide research into ice accretion, leading to improvements across multiple aircraft types. ATR's experience contributed to a deeper understanding of how turboprops interact with weather phenomena, benefiting aviation safety as a whole.

As technology advanced, ATR continued to integrate safety improvements into its upgrades. The ATR 72-500 introduced digital avionics that enhanced situational awareness for crews. Terrain awareness and warning systems (TAWS), traffic collision avoidance systems (TCAS), and more sophisticated autopilots became standard, reducing risks of controlled flight into terrain or mid-air collisions. With the ATR 72-600, safety was further strengthened through the Thales avionics suite, which gave pilots state-of-the-art tools for navigation, weather awareness, and flight management.

Another area of focus was survivability in accidents. ATR worked on structural enhancements to improve crashworthiness, such as energy-absorbing seats, reinforced fuselage structures, and improved fire suppression systems. While no aircraft manufacturer can eliminate the risk of accidents entirely, ATR's philosophy was to reduce risks as much as possible and to maximize survival chances when incidents did occur.

Maintenance practices formed the backbone of long-term reliability. ATR developed a network of maintenance, repair, and overhaul (MRO) facilities worldwide, ensuring that operators had access to parts and expertise. Maintenance schedules were optimized to reduce downtime while maintaining safety margins. ATR's global support network became a selling point, particularly in regions with less developed aviation infrastructure. Airlines knew that acquiring ATR aircraft meant gaining access to a manufacturer invested in keeping the fleet flying safely and reliably.

The commitment to safety also extended into the cargo versions of the ATR. With the introduction of the ATR 72-600F, new certification processes ensured that freighter-specific risks, such as cargo fire hazards, were addressed with modern suppression systems and reinforced compartments. ATR recognized that safety was just as critical in cargo operations as in passenger service, especially as e-commerce created increasing demand for dependable freighters.

Looking at the overall safety record, ATR aircraft have demonstrated rates consistent with industry averages for regional aviation. Given the sheer number of ATRs in operation worldwide—more than 1,600 delivered by the 2020s—their accident history reflects both the challenges of wide deployment and the success of continuous improvements. While early icing accidents tarnished the reputation temporarily, the decades since have shown that ATR aircraft are among the safest and most reliable regional turboprops in service.

The lessons learned from ATR's safety journey illustrate the resilience of the company's approach. Rather than deny or downplay challenges, ATR addressed them directly with technical modifications, operational procedures, and enhanced training. Each incident became a catalyst for progress, reinforcing ATR's long-term commitment to building safe and dependable aircraft. The company's openness to collaboration with regulators and operators ensured that improvements were based on rigorous analysis and practical application.

By the 2010s, ATR could credibly position its aircraft as not only efficient and versatile but also exceptionally safe and reliable. Airlines continued to invest in large fleets, confident that the lessons of the past had been absorbed and that ATR aircraft met the highest standards. The narrative of safety, once a challenge, became part of the company's strength, showing that even in aviation's most demanding sector—short-haul, regional, often in extreme environments—turboprops could be trusted to perform with resilience.

ATR's story of safety and reliability is, in many ways, a microcosm of the aviation industry itself: a journey of continuous learning, adaptation, and improvement. Through its experiences, ATR not only secured its own place in aviation history but also contributed to the broader advancement of safety in regional flight. As turboprops remain vital for connecting remote communities, flying into rugged airstrips, and serving as the backbone of short-haul aviation, the confidence in their safety and reliability stands as one of ATR's most enduring legacies.

Chapter 9: ATR and Environmental Efficiency

In the second half of the twentieth century, aircraft manufacturers were largely judged by their ability to deliver speed, range, and passenger capacity. Environmental considerations, while not entirely absent, rarely guided design priorities. By the 1980s, when ATR was formed, global aviation was still growing rapidly, with fuel costs and operational economics holding greater sway than carbon emissions or noise footprints. Yet, as environmental consciousness spread in the 1990s and accelerated into the twenty-first century, the aviation industry faced mounting pressure to address its contribution to climate change, urban noise, and local air quality. In this evolving context, ATR found itself in a unique position. The very nature of its turboprop aircraft—lightweight, efficient, and optimized for short-haul travel—allowed the company to align naturally with a new narrative: regional air travel that was not only practical but also more sustainable.

The efficiency advantage of turboprops over jets was neither incidental nor minor. Jet engines, particularly on regional jets, consumed significantly more fuel on routes under 500 nautical miles. These routes represented ATR's core market. Whereas a regional jet required higher thrust to climb quickly to cruising altitude and burned large amounts of fuel during the process, a turboprop's propeller-driven design allowed for more efficient energy transfer at the lower altitudes and shorter stages common in regional flying. ATR consistently demonstrated that its aircraft consumed up to 40 percent less fuel than comparable regional jets on short-haul missions. This translated into lower operating costs for airlines and, crucially, reduced emissions per passenger-kilometer.

As regulators, governments, and the public became more focused on carbon emissions, this advantage became a critical differentiator. ATR did not need to reinvent its aircraft to claim environmental efficiency; rather, it built on its existing strengths. Marketing materials increasingly emphasized fuel burn per seat, framing ATR not just as a cost-effective solution but as the environmentally responsible choice. Airlines found this argument particularly compelling when governments introduced taxes or incentives linked to emissions. For example, in European countries where environmental regulations were tightening, an ATR could be promoted as the airline's green option for domestic and short international routes.

Noise was another dimension of environmental performance where ATR gained traction. Turboprops traditionally generated lower noise footprints than jets, particularly during takeoff and landing. This mattered greatly in regional airports situated close to urban centers, where community noise complaints often restricted growth. ATR invested in propeller blade redesigns to further reduce noise levels, integrating six-blade propellers that distributed sound energy more evenly and produced less intrusive frequencies. The "whisper" branding associated with later ATRs underscored this selling point, enabling airlines to operate into noise-sensitive airports with fewer restrictions.

Environmental efficiency was not only about performance but also about perception. Airlines, especially national carriers and large regional operators, increasingly sought to demonstrate their commitment to sustainability. By operating ATR aircraft, they could highlight tangible reductions in fuel consumption and emissions, presenting themselves as aligned with broader environmental goals. ATR supported this positioning by publishing comparative data and working with independent bodies to validate its claims. In an era when passengers and governments were beginning to scrutinize aviation's environmental impact more closely, ATR aircraft became an important part of the narrative that aviation could be greener.

The 2000s brought a further sharpening of environmental debates. With the Kyoto Protocol signed in 1997 and implemented in subsequent years, governments worldwide committed to reducing greenhouse gas emissions. Aviation, while not immediately included in many national reduction targets, was identified as a growing source of emissions. Europe, in particular, became a focal point for regulatory pressure. The European Union Emissions Trading System (EU ETS), introduced in 2005 and extended to aviation in 2012, required airlines to account for their carbon emissions. Under this system, operators of fuel-efficient aircraft like ATR turboprops held a clear financial advantage. Lower emissions per flight meant fewer allowances to purchase, reinforcing ATR's pitch that efficiency was not only environmentally sound but also economically prudent.

ATR's environmental advantage was especially clear when comparing aircraft utilization. A regional airline flying multiple short hops daily could achieve substantial reductions in fuel consumption by operating ATRs instead of regional jets. For example, on a 300-kilometer sector, an ATR 72 might consume around 1,000 kilograms of fuel, while a comparable regional jet could burn 1,600 kilograms or more. Scaled across dozens of flights per day, the savings became significant in both cost and emissions. Airlines used these figures to justify fleet strategies that prioritized turboprops, particularly in markets where public scrutiny of aviation emissions was strongest.

Beyond aircraft design, ATR explored ways to embed environmental considerations into its broader operations. The company promoted "eco-efficiency" programs that encouraged airlines to optimize flight procedures, such as continuous descent approaches and reduced engine taxiing. ATR partnered with operators to implement these measures, positioning itself not just as a manufacturer but as a collaborator in reducing aviation's environmental footprint. These initiatives underscored a shift in the aviation industry: manufacturers were increasingly expected not only to build efficient aircraft but also to support airlines in achieving broader sustainability goals.

The push toward sustainability also intersected with evolving technology. ATR continually invested in avionics and systems upgrades that supported more precise flight management, reducing unnecessary fuel burn. Lighter cabin materials were introduced to cut overall weight, further improving efficiency. Even small changes, such as optimizing paint thickness or introducing more efficient lighting, contributed to the cumulative goal of reducing fuel consumption and emissions. These incremental improvements reflected ATR's philosophy of continuous refinement, ensuring that each new generation of its aircraft was more environmentally efficient than the last.

Another important dimension was the suitability of ATR aircraft for markets where environmental considerations intersected with social priorities. In regions such as the Pacific islands, Southeast Asia, and parts of Africa, ATRs provided vital connectivity while consuming less fuel and producing fewer emissions than alternative aircraft. This was not simply an economic advantage; it aligned with broader goals of sustainable development. By enabling essential air links with a smaller environmental footprint, ATR aircraft became part of national strategies to balance connectivity with ecological responsibility.

ATR also played an important role in shaping industry discourse around the future of sustainable aviation fuels (SAFs). As governments and industry stakeholders recognized that fuel efficiency alone would not achieve the carbon reductions needed to meet international targets, attention turned to SAFs derived from renewable sources. ATR actively supported certification programs for its aircraft to operate with blends of SAFs, ensuring compatibility with emerging fuels. Demonstration flights were conducted using biofuel blends, highlighting that ATR turboprops could contribute to decarbonization not only through efficiency but also through compatibility with new technologies.

By the 2010s, as climate change became a central political issue, ATR embraced a more explicit environmental branding. The company highlighted studies showing that on routes under 500 nautical miles, ATR aircraft emitted up to 45 percent less CO_2 per passenger than regional jets. This statistic became a cornerstone of marketing campaigns, resonating with both airlines and policymakers. Airlines in Europe, Asia, and Latin America began to cite ATR's environmental performance as a reason for fleet choices, emphasizing to their passengers that they were operating "eco-friendly" flights.

The COVID-19 pandemic of 2020 added new dimensions to the environmental debate. As aviation demand collapsed and governments discussed rebuilding the industry, calls for a "green recovery" gained momentum. Governments offering financial support to airlines often attached environmental conditions, requiring commitments to reduce emissions or modernize fleets with more efficient aircraft. ATR benefitted from this trend, as airlines seeking to demonstrate environmental responsibility turned to turboprops as a practical solution. In markets where regional connectivity was vital but budgets were strained, ATR aircraft offered a way to restore services while aligning with sustainability goals.

The conversation about environmental efficiency has also increasingly extended to life-cycle analysis—considering not only fuel consumption during operation but also emissions associated with manufacturing, maintenance, and end-of-life recycling. ATR, as part of Airbus and Leonardo, aligned with industry initiatives to improve recycling of aircraft materials and reduce the environmental impact of production. Efforts included using more sustainable materials in manufacturing and promoting recycling of retired aircraft components. By participating in these programs, ATR positioned itself as part of a holistic approach to sustainability, rather than focusing solely on fuel burn.

Technological innovation remains central to ATR's environmental vision for the future. Research into hybrid-electric propulsion and distributed energy systems offers possibilities for further reductions in emissions, particularly on short-haul flights where turboprops already excel. ATR has signaled openness to integrating such technologies when they become viable, continuing its tradition of incremental adaptation. The modular design of ATR aircraft, with proven adaptability for cargo, passenger, and special mission roles, provides a foundation for integrating new propulsion systems in the future.

ATR's environmental efficiency has not only shaped its commercial success but also its reputation. In a world increasingly attentive to the environmental consequences of air travel, ATR's aircraft are often described as the "green choice" for regional airlines. While turboprops may not match the glamour of sleek jets, their practicality and efficiency have become virtues in a sustainability-conscious era. This shift in values has allowed ATR to move beyond a defensive comparison with jets to a confident assertion of leadership in green aviation.

The numbers tell part of the story, but so too does the lived experience of communities served by ATR aircraft. In island nations where flights are short but essential, ATRs provide lifelines while consuming less fuel. In mountainous regions where environmental preservation is a priority, ATRs connect communities with less noise and pollution. In developed countries grappling with climate targets, ATRs enable airlines to continue operating regional networks while meeting environmental commitments. This intersection of economic, environmental, and social priorities has cemented ATR's place in the twenty-first century aviation landscape.

ATR's journey in environmental efficiency demonstrates the convergence of design philosophy, operational adaptability, and strategic communication. From the beginning, turboprops were efficient by necessity; they had to be competitive on short-haul routes where margins were tight. Over time, this efficiency became not only a business advantage but also an environmental imperative. By recognizing and amplifying this narrative, ATR transformed what could have been a niche advantage into a defining strength.

As the aviation industry faces mounting pressure to decarbonize, ATR's position remains strong. While long-haul jets struggle to identify radical solutions, regional aviation has already taken significant steps. ATR aircraft, with their proven efficiency and compatibility with emerging sustainable fuels, embody the possibility of an aviation sector that is both accessible and environmentally responsible. This alignment between technological reality and global environmental goals ensures that ATR remains not only relevant but also central to the debate about the future of flying.

In the decades ahead, environmental efficiency will not be an optional marketing theme but a core determinant of success in aviation. ATR's history of efficiency, its embrace of sustainability narratives, and its readiness to adapt position it well to continue shaping short-haul aviation. The company's quiet empire, built on turboprops, is also an empire of environmental pragmatism: proving that the future of flight can be efficient, reliable, and responsible.

Chapter 10: Ownership Shifts and Airbus Involvement

The story of ATR's ownership structure is inseparable from the broader consolidation of the European aerospace industry. From the moment Aérospatiale of France and Aeritalia of Italy created Avions de Transport Régional in 1981, the company's binational character became both a defining strength and a source of complexity. Over the years, as the parent companies themselves underwent mergers, restructurings, and integrations into larger industrial groups, ATR's ownership shifted accordingly. By the early twenty-first century, the once straightforward Franco-Italian partnership had evolved into a joint venture between two of Europe's largest aerospace powers: Airbus and Leonardo. Understanding this trajectory requires examining not only ATR's internal development but also the external forces reshaping European aviation, from political imperatives to economic pressures.

When ATR was founded, Aérospatiale and Aeritalia represented two of Europe's most prominent aerospace firms. Aérospatiale had been formed in 1970 through the merger of several French state-owned companies, consolidating expertise in both civil and military aviation. It was heavily involved in high-profile programs such as Concorde and Airbus, symbolizing France's ambition to maintain a leading role in global aerospace. Aeritalia, created in 1969 from Fiat Aviazione and Aerfer, represented Italy's principal aerospace company. Like Aérospatiale, it combined a focus on military aircraft with ambitions in the civil sector. The ATR joint venture was structured as a 50-50 partnership, reflecting the political importance of balance between the two nations. Each partner contributed production responsibilities—France overseeing final assembly in Toulouse, Italy managing significant portions of fuselage and wing production in Naples.

For much of the 1980s and 1990s, this arrangement provided stability. ATR's products found success worldwide, and the profits were shared equally between the partners. But behind the scenes, the European aerospace industry was undergoing dramatic transformation. The fragmented landscape of national champions was increasingly seen as inefficient in a global marketplace dominated by massive American firms like Boeing and McDonnell Douglas. European governments pushed for consolidation to achieve economies of scale and strengthen competitiveness. This process ultimately reshaped ATR's ownership.

The first major shift came in 1990, when Aeritalia merged with Selenia, an Italian electronics company, to form Alenia Aeronautica. This new entity became Italy's primary aerospace firm, operating as part of the state-owned conglomerate Finmeccanica. ATR's Italian stake thus passed from Aeritalia to Alenia, but the operational structure of the joint venture remained unchanged. France's Aérospatiale continued as the other half of the partnership.

A more dramatic transformation occurred on the French side. In 2000, Aérospatiale merged with several German and Spanish companies to form the European Aeronautic Defence and Space Company (EADS). This massive merger created a pan-European giant, consolidating Airbus as its primary commercial aircraft division. ATR, as part of Aérospatiale's civil portfolio, became part of EADS by extension. From that moment, ATR's French ownership was effectively held through Airbus, even though the joint venture retained its own legal and operational identity.

These developments created a new dynamic. ATR was no longer just a partnership between a French and an Italian national company; it was a joint venture between Alenia, a subsidiary of Finmeccanica, and EADS, a multinational conglomerate with Airbus at its core. While ATR continued to operate from its Toulouse headquarters, the decision-making process now involved larger corporate structures with their own priorities. This shift introduced both opportunities and challenges. On one hand, ATR could leverage the global marketing power of Airbus and benefit from synergies in procurement and technology. On the other hand, ATR risked being overshadowed by Airbus's massive commercial jet programs, which dominated attention and resources within EADS.

Despite these challenges, ATR managed to maintain its distinct identity. The company continued to focus exclusively on regional turboprops, leaving Airbus free to concentrate on jets. This clear division of labor avoided direct competition between the two entities and allowed ATR to carve out a specialized niche. At the same time, ATR benefitted from Airbus's global reach. Sales campaigns were often supported by Airbus's worldwide network, giving ATR access to markets where it might otherwise have struggled to establish a presence.

The Italian side of the partnership also evolved. Finmeccanica, which had taken control of Alenia, restructured multiple times during the early 2000s, consolidating its aerospace and defense businesses. Alenia Aeronautica remained the Italian shareholder in ATR, continuing to oversee significant production in Naples and other Italian sites. This arrangement ensured that ATR remained a truly binational program, with political support in both countries tied to local employment and industrial participation.

The balance between Airbus (through EADS) and Alenia occasionally created tensions. Airbus was vastly larger and more influential, with global brand recognition far exceeding ATR's. Some observers wondered whether Airbus might one day absorb ATR fully, integrating it into its portfolio. However, Alenia consistently defended its 50 percent stake, viewing ATR as a strategically important foothold in the civil aircraft market. This determination preserved the joint venture structure, even as Airbus's dominance in European aerospace grew.

In 2016, EADS rebranded itself as Airbus Group, further cementing the Airbus name as the centerpiece of its identity. ATR thus became officially co-owned by Airbus Group and Alenia Aermacchi, the successor of Alenia Aeronautica after another internal reorganization. That same year, Finmeccanica rebranded itself as Leonardo, simplifying its structure and presenting a more cohesive global identity. ATR's ownership was therefore clarified: 50 percent Airbus, 50 percent Leonardo. This Franco-Italian equilibrium, maintained for more than three decades, had survived waves of industrial change.

The involvement of Airbus proved particularly beneficial in marketing. Airbus's global network of sales and support offices provided ATR with unprecedented reach. Airlines considering ATR turboprops were often existing Airbus customers for larger jets, making cross-selling opportunities attractive. Airbus could present airlines with a full range of solutions, from ATR turboprops for regional routes to widebody jets for long-haul operations. This synergy strengthened ATR's competitiveness against rivals like Bombardier, which lacked such extensive global backing.

Technical collaboration also offered advantages. While ATR retained its own engineering teams, it had access to Airbus expertise in avionics, materials, and systems integration. Over the years, incremental upgrades to ATR aircraft often drew on Airbus technologies, ensuring commonality and enhancing customer confidence. In maintenance and training, too, Airbus's involvement provided scale. ATR operators could benefit from training facilities and support infrastructure integrated into Airbus's global network.

Yet, the relationship was not without its difficulties. Within Airbus, ATR remained a small player compared to the massive revenues generated by commercial jets. At times, ATR executives expressed concern that their needs were overshadowed by Airbus's focus on larger programs like the A320 and A350. Ensuring sufficient investment for ATR's product development required persistent advocacy, both within Airbus and in negotiations with Leonardo. For its part,

Leonardo also had its own priorities, particularly in defense and helicopters, which sometimes diverted attention away from ATR. The joint venture structure thus required constant balancing of interests.

Despite these complexities, ATR's ownership structure proved remarkably durable. The binational character of the company provided resilience. Neither Airbus nor Leonardo could unilaterally dictate strategy, requiring consensus decisions that ensured continued support for ATR's turboprops. While this occasionally slowed decision-making, it also prevented radical shifts that might have jeopardized the company's stability. The political dimension was equally important. French and Italian governments valued ATR not only as an industrial success but also as a symbol of European cooperation. Maintaining joint ownership ensured continued employment and technological expertise in both countries, securing political goodwill.

As Airbus deepened its involvement, ATR also benefited from the broader trend of regional specialization within the global aerospace industry. Rather than competing directly with Airbus's jets, ATR occupied a complementary niche. This strategic clarity helped preserve its relevance. Airlines understood that ATR turboprops were not an afterthought but a core product line, backed by the marketing power of Airbus and the engineering expertise of both partners.

The significance of Airbus's involvement extended beyond sales and engineering to strategic positioning in the environmental and regulatory landscape. As discussions about aviation's carbon footprint intensified, ATR found its messaging amplified by Airbus's broader sustainability campaigns. Airbus's commitment to developing new propulsion technologies, including hybrid-electric concepts, reinforced ATR's own narrative of efficiency. The alignment between ATR's turboprop efficiency and Airbus's long-term environmental vision created a coherent European stance on sustainable aviation.

Financially, the joint venture structure allowed ATR to operate with a degree of independence while benefiting from the backing of two major aerospace groups. Profits were shared between Airbus and Leonardo, providing steady returns that justified continued investment. At the same time, ATR was not burdened by the massive research and development costs associated with large jet programs. This balance made ATR an attractive asset for both shareholders, contributing to their civil aerospace portfolios without excessive financial risk.

The ownership shifts and Airbus involvement also influenced ATR's corporate culture. While ATR maintained its own identity, the presence of Airbus fostered a more global outlook. The company's executives were often drawn from both parent organizations, bringing diverse perspectives. This interchange of personnel created a dynamic environment where French, Italian, and broader European influences converged. The result was a corporate culture that valued collaboration and adaptability, traits essential for surviving in the competitive regional aircraft market.

By the 2010s, ATR had become firmly established as the world's leading turboprop manufacturer, with a market share exceeding 70 percent in its segment. This success owed much to the stability and resources provided by its ownership structure. The combination of Airbus's global scale and Leonardo's commitment to maintaining a presence in civil aviation created a powerful foundation. While rivals like Bombardier struggled and eventually exited the turboprop market by selling the Dash 8 program to De Havilland Canada, ATR's joint venture remained robust.

Looking at the broader historical arc, ATR's ownership journey reflects the evolution of European aerospace integration. From national companies defending their autonomy in the 1980s, Europe moved toward multinational structures in the 1990s and 2000s. ATR adapted to these shifts while preserving its binational character. The partnership between Airbus and Leonardo represents not only industrial collaboration but also political symbolism: a demonstration that European nations can share ownership and responsibility for a global industrial success.

The quiet endurance of ATR's ownership model contrasts with the turbulence often associated with aerospace mergers. While many programs suffered from disputes over control, ATR managed to sustain equilibrium. This stability allowed the company to focus on its core mission: delivering efficient, reliable turboprop aircraft to airlines worldwide. The Airbus connection enhanced credibility and market access, while the Leonardo stake ensured continuity of Italian industrial participation. Together, these elements formed a partnership that has endured far longer than many industry observers might have expected.

In the decades ahead, the question of ownership will remain important. As Airbus pursues new technologies and Leonardo refines its portfolio, ATR's place within their strategies will continue to evolve. Yet, the history of the joint venture suggests resilience. The company's success is not solely the result of aircraft design but also of the unique balance of ownership that has preserved its identity while providing access to global resources. In this sense, ATR's ownership story is itself a testament to European cooperation—an enduring alliance that has shaped not only the company's fortunes but also the landscape of regional aviation.

Chapter 11: The Asian Ascendancy

ATR's story in Asia-Pacific is one of extraordinary expansion, shaped by geography, demography, and economics. No other region embraced the turboprop manufacturer's philosophy of short-haul efficiency as enthusiastically as Asia, and no other region so clearly demonstrated the indispensable role of regional aviation in modern development. From the mid-1980s onward, Asia-Pacific emerged not only as a lucrative market but also as a defining arena for ATR's identity. The company's turboprops, first the ATR 42 and then the larger ATR 72, became central to connecting sprawling archipelagos, mountainous interiors, and densely populated regions where jets were uneconomical or impractical. By the 2010s, Asia had become ATR's single largest market, accounting for more than half of its global fleet in operation.

The reasons for ATR's dominance in Asia can be traced first to geography. Indonesia, the Philippines, and other island nations posed unique challenges for aviation. With thousands of islands, many of them separated by stretches of water too long for ferries yet too short for jet services, the need for short-hop connectivity was immense. Airstrips were often modest in size and lacked the infrastructure for larger aircraft. ATR turboprops, with their ability to operate from short runways, low fuel burn, and resilience in hot and humid climates, were ideally suited for such conditions. Jets struggled to serve these routes economically, leaving a clear gap in the market that ATR filled with precision.

Indonesia became the archetype of ATR's Asian success story. With more than 17,000 islands spread across 5,000 kilometers, the country posed one of the most formidable transportation challenges in the world. Road and rail networks were often limited to individual islands, leaving air travel as the only practical means of connection. Beginning in the late 1980s and accelerating through the 1990s, Indonesian carriers began to adopt ATRs for inter-island services. Merpati Nusantara, Garuda Indonesia's regional subsidiary, was an early customer, using the aircraft to reach secondary and tertiary destinations across the archipelago. Over time, as Indonesia's aviation market liberalized, low-cost carriers and regional operators alike embraced the ATR. Lion Air, which grew into one of Asia's largest airlines, established its regional arm, Wings Air, with a fleet built almost entirely around ATR 72s. By the late 2010s, Wings Air had become the single largest operator of ATR aircraft in the world, with well over 60 units in service. This fleet enabled Wings Air to connect small communities from Sumatra to Papua, places that might otherwise have remained isolated from the economic dynamism of Indonesia's major cities.

The Philippines provided another dramatic stage for ATR's ascendancy. Like Indonesia, it is an archipelago nation, with more than 7,000 islands. While Manila and Cebu acted as major hubs, vast swaths of the country required smaller aircraft to link provincial capitals and remote towns. Cebu Pacific Air, one of the Philippines' dominant low-cost carriers, established a regional subsidiary, Cebgo, to handle these routes. Cebgo operated ATRs extensively, making them a familiar sight across the islands. The aircraft's ability to land on short runways and its low operating costs were crucial in sustaining services to destinations where jets would have been uneconomic. By deploying ATRs, Cebu Pacific not only strengthened its domestic network but also fulfilled a broader social role, ensuring that peripheral communities remained connected to the nation's economic and cultural life.

India, though not an island nation, presented a different but equally compelling case for ATR's role in Asia. With a population exceeding one billion and a rapidly growing economy, India faced immense demand for air travel. However, much of this demand arose not in the megacities of Delhi or Mumbai, but in smaller regional centers. The Indian government recognized the importance of improving connectivity to these underserved cities and towns, launching the Regional Connectivity Scheme, known as UDAN, in 2017. ATR became the natural choice for airlines participating in this program. SpiceJet and IndiGo, India's two largest carriers, both established regional subsidiaries that deployed ATR 72s extensively. The aircraft's economics allowed them to operate thin routes profitably, linking places such as Shillong, Jabalpur, and Tirupati to larger hubs. By the early 2020s, India had become one of ATR's most promising growth markets, with dozens of aircraft ordered specifically to meet the demand generated by UDAN.

Beyond these flagship markets, ATR established strong presences across Asia-Pacific. In Thailand, Bangkok Airways operated ATRs to destinations across the Gulf of Thailand and into neighboring Cambodia and Myanmar. In Vietnam,

Vietnam Airlines and its regional arm deployed ATRs for domestic services, though eventually shifting toward jets as infrastructure improved. In Myanmar, Air KBZ and Mann Yadanarpon Airlines used ATRs to connect Yangon with secondary cities. Across the Pacific, carriers in Papua New Guinea, Fiji, and other island states adopted ATRs as the backbone of their fleets, relying on the aircraft's ruggedness to handle demanding operating environments.

One of the most important factors underpinning ATR's Asian success was the alignment between its aircraft characteristics and the financial realities of regional airlines. Many Asian carriers operated in markets where fares were low and competition intense. Cost efficiency was therefore paramount. ATR's turboprops, burning significantly less fuel than regional jets over short sectors, offered unmatched economics. Airlines could operate ATRs with lower break-even loads, making routes viable that would otherwise have been impossible. In countries where per-capita income limited fare levels, this efficiency was not just an advantage but a necessity.

The ability to operate in challenging environments further reinforced ATR's value. Many Asian airports had short runways, basic navigation aids, and limited ground handling infrastructure. ATR's design, with excellent short-field performance and robust systems, allowed it to thrive under such conditions. In places like Papua New Guinea, where mountainous terrain made aviation both essential and hazardous, ATRs proved their worth by safely serving demanding routes. In Indonesia and the Philippines, their ability to land on remote island airstrips without elaborate facilities made them indispensable.

The growth of low-cost carriers in Asia also played a decisive role. As budget airlines proliferated across the region in the 2000s and 2010s, they sought ways to extend their networks into smaller markets without undermining their low-cost model. ATR turboprops provided the perfect solution. Cebu Pacific, Lion Air, and SpiceJet all created regional arms using ATRs, integrating turboprop operations into their broader networks. This strategy allowed them to capture traffic from smaller cities and feed it into their mainline jet services, expanding their customer base and enhancing connectivity. ATR's aircraft, with their proven reliability and straightforward maintenance, fit seamlessly into these hybrid models.

The social and political impact of ATR's presence in Asia cannot be overstated. By connecting remote communities, the aircraft helped promote national integration and economic development. In countries with vast geographic divides, ATR flights were often more than commercial services—they were lifelines. In Indonesia, for example, ATRs linked the central government in Jakarta with remote provinces, fostering cohesion in a diverse and sprawling nation. In India, ATR flights under UDAN brought modern air connectivity to towns that had never before seen scheduled air services, reducing travel times dramatically and integrating them into the national economy.

ATR's success in Asia also reflected the company's ability to adapt to regional needs. The manufacturer established training and support facilities across the region, ensuring that airlines could maintain high standards of safety and efficiency. In Singapore, ATR created a training center with full flight simulators, serving as a hub for Asian operators. This commitment to localized support reassured airlines that they would not be left struggling with maintenance or training challenges. It also demonstrated ATR's recognition that Asia was not merely a sales territory but the core of its global market.

As ATR's footprint expanded, the company became closely identified with the Asian aviation story. By the late 2010s, it was estimated that more than 40 percent of ATR flights worldwide occurred in Asia-Pacific. The region had become not only ATR's largest customer base but also its most important proving ground. Airlines operating ATRs in Asia demonstrated the aircraft's versatility to the world, showcasing how turboprops could serve everything from high-frequency commuter routes to lifeline services for isolated villages.

Competition was not absent. Bombardier's Dash 8 series also made inroads in Asia, particularly in markets where slightly higher speed was valued. However, ATR's lower costs and better availability of support infrastructure gave it the edge. The Dash 8's eventual decline left ATR as the undisputed leader in the turboprop segment, with little serious competition. Jets, while attractive for trunk routes, simply could not match ATR's economics on short hops. This market dynamic entrenched ATR's dominance.

The narrative of ATR in Asia also underscores the broader role of aviation in economic development. As Asia's economies grew rapidly in the late twentieth and early twenty-first centuries, infrastructure development often lagged behind demand. ATRs provided an immediate solution, delivering connectivity without requiring the construction of long runways or sophisticated terminals. In effect, the aircraft allowed air networks to leapfrog traditional infrastructure constraints, accelerating integration and development.

By the 2020s, ATR had become an integral part of the fabric of Asian aviation. Whether in the vast archipelago of Indonesia, the crowded skies of India, or the island chains of the Philippines, ATR turboprops were omnipresent. They carried commuters, tourists, students, and traders, weaving together nations and regions with unmatched efficiency. In doing so, they fulfilled the vision of their creators: to provide a reliable, economical aircraft tailored to the realities of regional air travel. Asia, more than any other region, demonstrated just how powerful that vision could be.

Chapter 12: African Lifelines

Africa has long been described as a continent of vast distances and limited infrastructure, where the challenge of connecting communities goes beyond the conventional boundaries of transport policy. In this environment, aviation plays an indispensable role, bridging gaps that road, rail, or waterborne transport cannot feasibly cover. Within this story, ATR has carved a particularly vital place, its turboprops becoming synonymous with regional connectivity across Africa. From the dusty strips of the Sahel to the lush equatorial jungles and the busy commuter corridors of southern Africa, ATR's presence has been felt in the lives of millions. What distinguishes ATR's African story is not simply market share but the unique way its aircraft became lifelines, enabling essential links for healthcare, education, commerce, and governance in places where no other means of regular connection could serve so effectively.

The emergence of ATR in Africa coincided with major transformations on the continent in the 1980s and 1990s. As nations gained independence and sought to develop national carriers, aviation became both a symbol of sovereignty and a tool for integration. Yet many African countries faced daunting economic realities: low per-capita incomes, dispersed populations, and rudimentary infrastructure. These conditions demanded aircraft that were affordable to operate, easy to maintain, and capable of landing on short or unimproved runways. The ATR 42, launched in 1984, and the larger ATR 72, which followed in 1988, offered precisely the characteristics African operators required. Their turboprop efficiency, simple design philosophy, and ability to handle challenging conditions positioned them as natural choices for airlines navigating Africa's unique geography and economics.

Early adoption came from West and Central Africa, where national airlines were tasked with connecting distant provincial centers. Air Burkina, Air Sénégal, and Cameroon Airlines became among the first ATR operators on the continent, flying the ATR 42 into regional airports that had previously seen few or no scheduled services. The type's ruggedness was a major attraction. Runways in Ouagadougou or Banjul might be paved, but secondary destinations often had short strips with minimal navigation aids. ATR's ability to take off and land on runways as short as 1,100 meters allowed airlines to reach communities that jets could not, ensuring that far-flung regions were not left isolated from national life.

As the 1990s unfolded, more African operators turned to ATR, driven both by economics and by necessity. South African Express, a subsidiary of South African Airways, introduced ATR 42s and ATR 72s into its fleet to connect Johannesburg with smaller cities across the country and neighboring states. In Nigeria, the continent's most populous country, airlines such as Overland Airways and Arik Air relied heavily on ATRs to provide frequent, affordable connections between Lagos, Abuja, and secondary cities. Overland Airways in particular built its entire business model around ATR turboprops, operating them on domestic and regional routes with a strong emphasis on reliability and accessibility.

Nowhere, however, did ATR find a role as critical as in East Africa. Kenya Airways, the region's flagship carrier, at one time operated ATRs to link Nairobi with smaller Kenyan towns and regional capitals. More enduring, however, was the example of Precision Air in Tanzania. Founded in the early 1990s, Precision Air grew from a modest charter outfit into a major scheduled carrier, with ATRs forming the backbone of its fleet. The aircraft allowed the airline to establish dense domestic networks linking Dar es Salaam, Arusha, Mwanza, and other towns, while also venturing into neighboring countries. In a nation with vast rural areas and limited road networks, ATR flights became vital arteries of commerce and tourism. They carried local traders to urban markets, students to universities, and tourists to Serengeti airstrips, integrating Tanzania in ways no other mode of transport could match.

The suitability of ATR aircraft to Africa's environment was not accidental but deeply rooted in their design. Turboprops inherently offered better fuel economy on the short sectors that dominate African aviation. With fuel costs often representing the single largest expense for local airlines—and with supply chains for aviation fuel sometimes fragile—this efficiency was critical. Furthermore, ATR's engines, propellers, and systems were proven in hot-and-high conditions, enabling safe operation from airports such as Addis Ababa or Johannesburg where density altitude challenged many aircraft types. The robust landing gear and forgiving handling qualities of the ATR family also allowed pilots to operate from semi-prepared runways in remote communities without excessive wear and tear on the aircraft.

As globalization accelerated in the 2000s, ATR's importance in Africa grew. The liberalization of African aviation under initiatives like the Yamoussoukro Decision in 1999 sought to open skies between countries, creating opportunities for regional carriers. ATR-equipped airlines were well positioned to take advantage of these new freedoms. As cross-border services expanded, ATR turboprops became common sights at secondary airports across West, Central, and East Africa, linking places like Accra to Abidjan, Douala to Libreville, or Kigali to Entebbe. These were not just commercial routes but vital enablers of regional integration, supporting trade blocs such as the Economic Community of West African States (ECOWAS) and the East African Community (EAC).

The aircraft also played an essential role in humanitarian and governmental operations. Non-governmental organizations and United Nations agencies frequently chartered ATRs to deliver aid, transport personnel, or conduct monitoring missions. Their ability to operate in austere conditions made them invaluable during crises, from conflict zones in Central Africa to disaster response in Mozambique or Madagascar. The ATR's blend of reliability, simplicity, and efficiency meant that it could support missions where larger aircraft were impractical or uneconomic.

While ATRs became lifelines for connectivity, their presence in Africa was not without challenges. Safety and reliability were constant concerns across the continent's aviation sector. Limited infrastructure, challenging weather patterns, and uneven regulatory oversight created difficulties for all operators, including those flying ATRs. Notable accidents, such as the 2000 crash of Kenya Airways Flight 431 (an Airbus A310, though it influenced regional safety culture) and subsequent ATR-related incidents in other carriers, underscored the urgent need for improved safety practices. ATR worked closely with African regulators and airlines to provide training, support, and technical guidance, helping to raise operational standards. Training centers and maintenance partnerships were developed to ensure that African operators had access to the expertise necessary to maintain high safety levels.

By the 2010s, Africa had become one of ATR's strongest growth regions, with more than 120 aircraft in operation across nearly 30 airlines. Operators ranged from large, well-known carriers such as Ethiopian Airlines—whose regional affiliate, Ethiopian Mozambique Airlines, used ATRs extensively—to smaller carriers like Air Botswana and Air Madagascar. This widespread adoption reflected not only the aircraft's adaptability but also its economic indispensability. African airlines operated on thin margins in competitive environments. The ATR's lower break-even load compared to jets meant that even routes with modest demand could remain viable, sustaining connectivity that was critical to national cohesion and development.

The ATR's role in Africa also highlights the broader social and political significance of regional aviation. For many communities, the arrival of an ATR flight meant access to healthcare, education, and commerce that would otherwise have been out of reach. A patient from a rural province in

Gabon could be transported quickly to a hospital in Libreville. A student in Malawi could reach Lilongwe or Blantyre in hours rather than days. Traders in northern Ghana could bring goods to Accra efficiently. In each case, ATR aircraft played a tangible role in improving livelihoods.

The importance of ATRs extended to fostering tourism, a vital economic sector for many African nations. Countries like Tanzania, Kenya, and South Africa relied heavily on tourism revenue, and ATRs were crucial in linking remote safari lodges, game reserves, and coastal resorts to mainline hubs. Without the ability to transport visitors efficiently to these destinations, the tourism sector's growth would have been severely constrained. ATR flights thus supported both national economies and local employment in regions that depended heavily on tourist inflows.

An equally important dimension of ATR's African story is durability. Many aircraft remained in service for decades, passing from one operator to another in a thriving secondary market. This longevity was essential for airlines that could not afford constant fleet renewal. Leasing companies and brokers facilitated the transfer of used ATRs to African operators, ensuring a steady supply of affordable aircraft. In some cases, aircraft built in the 1980s were still flying scheduled services in Africa three decades later, a testament to their rugged design and adaptability.

By the early 2020s, ATR aircraft were operating in nearly every corner of Africa. From the deserts of Mauritania to the highlands of Ethiopia and the islands of the Seychelles, ATRs were a common presence. The company's market share in the turboprop segment across Africa regularly exceeded 70 percent, reflecting its dominance. This widespread deployment underscored the degree to which ATR had become not merely a supplier of aircraft but a partner in Africa's development journey.

As Africa looks to the future, with rapid population growth, urbanization, and economic diversification on the horizon, the role of ATR appears set to continue. The need for regional connectivity remains immense, and the constraints of infrastructure, cost, and geography persist. Jets will serve trunk routes between major cities, but turboprops will remain indispensable for secondary and tertiary links. ATR, with its unmatched track record and entrenched presence, is well positioned to sustain and expand its role as Africa's aviation lifeline.

In many ways, the story of ATR in Africa encapsulates the essence of the company's global mission. The aircraft are not simply machines ferrying passengers; they are enablers of mobility, integration, and opportunity. In the African context, this role becomes especially clear. ATRs have bridged the vast spaces of the continent, linking people and places that might otherwise remain isolated. They have supported governments, empowered businesses, and transformed daily lives. And in doing so, they have demonstrated the profound impact that a well-designed regional aircraft can have on human development.

Chapter 13: Latin America and the Caribbean Connection

If there is a region outside of Europe where the ATR family found perhaps its most natural habitat, it is Latin America and the Caribbean. Across a landscape defined by towering mountains, dense jungles, sprawling coastlines, and scattered islands, the ATR turboprops proved indispensable in knitting together communities that would otherwise remain fragmented. While jets carried passengers on long-haul links between major cities, ATRs excelled in the short-haul, high-frequency sectors that defined everyday mobility in Latin America. The story of ATR in this region is not merely one of commercial success but of necessity, as the aircraft became central to the flow of people, goods, and ideas across diverse geographies.

The first ATRs entered Latin America in the late 1980s, a time when many national carriers were struggling with financial constraints and economic turbulence. Debt crises, currency fluctuations, and political transitions all weighed heavily on the aviation sector. Yet despite these difficulties, the demand for regional connectivity remained strong. Populations in countries like Colombia, Brazil, and Mexico were dispersed across multiple urban centers, each requiring air links to sustain commerce and national integration. The ATR 42, with its modest size and ability to operate from short runways, was a natural fit. Airlines in Colombia, including SAM (Sociedad Aeronáutica de Medellín) and Avianca's regional affiliates, were among the first to adopt the ATR 42, using it to link

Bogotá with smaller Andean cities where airports were perched at high altitudes and hemmed in by mountains.

Colombia offered an ideal proving ground for ATR's capabilities. Cities such as Manizales, Armenia, and Popayán could not support large jet aircraft due to runway length and surrounding terrain. Turboprops were essential, and ATR's fuel efficiency gave it a cost advantage over competing models. The ATR 42 quickly proved it could handle steep approaches and challenging conditions, cementing its place in Colombian aviation. As Avianca consolidated its position as the country's flag carrier, ATR turboprops became embedded in its domestic network, ensuring reliable connections across the Andes.

In Brazil, the sheer size of the country presented an entirely different challenge. With more than 8.5 million square kilometers of territory, regional air travel was essential for binding together distant states. While the major cities of São Paulo, Rio de Janeiro, and Brasília were linked by dense jet networks, secondary and tertiary cities depended on regional aircraft. TAM Airlines (before its later merger with LAN to form LATAM) introduced ATR 42s and later ATR 72s into its fleet, connecting interior cities to its hubs. In the Amazon region, where rivers, forests, and limited roads made surface travel impractical, ATRs were vital for mobility. Manaus, the capital of Amazonas state, became a hub for ATR operations, with flights radiating out to remote communities deep in the rainforest. These flights carried not only passengers but also mail, medicine, and supplies, effectively serving as lifelines for settlements scattered along the Amazon River.

The Caribbean provided another natural arena for ATR's strengths. The region's geography, defined by short inter-island hops often less than 300 kilometers in length, played perfectly to the ATR's advantages. Airlines such as LIAT (Leeward Islands Air Transport) built their business models almost entirely around ATRs. From its base in Antigua, LIAT operated ATR 42s and ATR 72s to more than a dozen destinations, ranging from Puerto Rico in the north to Guyana in the south. The aircraft proved indispensable in connecting island nations with populations too small to support jets, enabling the free movement of citizens, tourists, and cargo. For decades, ATRs became the face of inter-island travel in the eastern Caribbean, where they were as common as ferries or buses in linking communities.

Similarly, in the French overseas territories of Martinique, Guadeloupe, and French Guiana, Air Caraïbes and Air Antilles relied heavily on ATR turboprops. These carriers not only provided vital domestic connections but also linked the territories with neighboring islands, reinforcing cultural and economic ties across the region. The aircraft's efficiency was particularly important in these markets, where ticket prices needed to remain accessible for local populations. ATR's lower operating costs meant that airlines could sustain frequent services even when demand fluctuated seasonally, such as during the tourist high season or holiday periods.

Mexico also became an important ATR market, particularly through regional carriers serving areas with difficult terrain.

Aeromar, one of Mexico's oldest continuously operating airlines, adopted ATRs as the backbone of its fleet. From its base in Mexico City, Aeromar operated ATR 42s and later ATR 72s to regional cities such as Veracruz, Oaxaca, and Puebla. These routes were typically under an hour in length, precisely the kind of sector where jets were uneconomical but where surface transport would take far longer. Aeromar's identity became closely tied to ATRs, with the airline operating dozens of examples over the years and even serving as a launch customer for updated ATR models.

The ATR's adaptability to Latin American geography extended well beyond the Caribbean and Mexico. In Chile, for instance, Aerovías DAP used ATRs to connect Punta Arenas with remote Patagonian communities, including those in Tierra del Fuego. These flights often operated in extreme weather conditions, with strong winds, freezing temperatures, and challenging visibility. Yet ATR aircraft proved resilient, allowing communities at the edge of the continent to remain linked to the outside world. Similarly, in Peru, where the Andes cut across the nation and make surface travel arduous, ATRs connected cities such as Cuzco and Arequipa with Lima and smaller provincial towns. In such environments, the aircraft's ability to operate safely at high-altitude airports was crucial.

By the early 2000s, ATR's presence in Latin America and the Caribbean was firmly established. More than 150 aircraft were operating across the region, with orders continuing to grow. What set ATR apart from competitors was not merely its aircraft performance but its economic suitability. Many airlines in Latin America operated under financial pressure, facing high fuel costs, currency volatility, and thin profit margins. The ATR's low fuel consumption and reduced maintenance costs provided a lifeline, allowing routes that might otherwise be unprofitable to remain viable. This economic advantage was reinforced by the aircraft's longevity. Many ATRs remained in service for decades, often passing from larger carriers to smaller regional airlines or charter operators, ensuring that the aircraft's utility extended well beyond its initial operator.

The aircraft's significance went beyond economics into the social fabric of the region. In the Caribbean, ATR flights were essential for family and cultural ties. Inter-island marriages, business ventures, and healthcare needs all depended on accessible air links. A passenger flying from St. Lucia to Dominica might be visiting relatives, while another traveling from Guadeloupe to Martinique might be seeking specialized medical treatment. In each case, ATR turboprops made these connections possible. The same applied in Latin America, where ATRs often served as shuttles for students, doctors, and small business owners, ensuring that national integration was not limited to major cities alone.

Tourism, a pillar of many regional economies, also benefited enormously from ATR operations. Resorts in the Caribbean and eco-tourism destinations in Latin America relied on ATRs to deliver visitors from hubs to final destinations. Without ATR flights, reaching places like St. Vincent, Dominica, or the Galápagos Islands would have been far more complicated, requiring multiple connections or long ferry rides. The aircraft's role in enabling tourism had direct economic consequences, supporting jobs in hotels, restaurants, and local businesses.

ATR's regional importance also extended to cargo. Even before the rise of dedicated freighter versions, ATRs in Latin America were routinely used to carry mixed loads of passengers and freight. Farmers in remote regions shipped produce to urban markets, while small manufacturers moved goods between cities. This dual-use capacity added to the aircraft's utility, particularly in countries with dispersed agricultural economies such as Brazil and Colombia. The eventual introduction of passenger-to-freighter conversions expanded this role further, with ATRs taking on dedicated cargo operations across the region.

By the 2010s, ATR's position in Latin America and the Caribbean was further consolidated through strategic partnerships. Maintenance and training centers were established in Brazil, Mexico, and the Caribbean to support growing fleets. ATR also worked closely with leasing companies to ensure a steady flow of aircraft to the region, recognizing that many carriers preferred leasing over outright purchase due to financial constraints. These initiatives helped cement ATR's long-term presence, ensuring that airlines could count on reliable support.

Even as regional jets became more common in Latin America, ATR maintained its relevance. Jets offered speed and comfort on longer routes, but they could not compete with ATR's economics on shorter sectors or its ability to operate from short and narrow runways. As a result, many airlines adopted mixed fleets, using jets for trunk routes and ATRs for feeder services. This dual strategy reinforced the aircraft's indispensability, as it filled a niche that jets could not.

ATR's dominance was particularly evident in markets like Colombia and the Caribbean, where the majority of regional turboprops were ATRs. By the mid-2010s, more than 70 percent of the turboprop fleet in the region carried the ATR badge. This dominance reflected not only the aircraft's suitability but also the company's commitment to building relationships with local carriers. ATR executives frequently visited the region, participated in airshows such as FIDAE in Chile, and engaged directly with airline leadership to understand their needs.

As of the early 2020s, ATR remained the undisputed leader in regional turboprops in Latin America and the Caribbean, with more than 200 aircraft in service. From the Andean highlands to the Caribbean Sea, ATRs were a common sight, often serving routes that no other aircraft could sustain. Their role extended far beyond aviation economics—they were integral to the very functioning of regional societies. Whether carrying passengers across short island hops, connecting isolated Amazonian towns, or shuttling cargo between provincial markets, ATR turboprops were woven into the daily life of the region.

The ATR story in Latin America and the Caribbean underscores the universal truth that geography shapes aviation. The aircraft succeeded here not because of chance but because its design aligned perfectly with the region's needs. Efficiency, versatility, and durability made it a natural solution for fragmented geographies and constrained economies. And in providing this solution, ATR did more than secure a market—it helped knit together nations, sustain communities, and expand opportunities across one of the most diverse regions on Earth.

Chapter 14: The Market for Second-Hand ATRs

One of the most remarkable aspects of the ATR story is not only its production success but the endurance of its aircraft well beyond their initial operators. If the first three decades of ATR's history were defined by the development and expansion of the ATR 42 and ATR 72 families across global passenger markets, the following decades highlighted another layer of resilience: the thriving secondary market. Unlike many aircraft that fade quickly after their first owners retire them, ATRs have consistently found new homes, extending their operational life by decades. This phenomenon became a defining element of the company's legacy, cementing the aircraft's reputation not just as efficient machines but as long-term investments that generate value across multiple ownership cycles.

The appeal of second-hand ATRs stems from a combination of durability, adaptability, and economic pragmatism. Turboprops by their nature are built to withstand rugged operations, short runway cycles, and frequent takeoffs and landings. ATR engineers designed their airframes and engines with these stresses in mind, resulting in aircraft that could handle thousands of flight hours without excessive wear. Over time, this durability proved to be one of the strongest selling points in the resale market. Airlines that could not afford brand-new aircraft often looked to the second-hand market for affordable, reliable solutions. In many cases, the choice was between acquiring a used ATR or not being able to operate at all.

From the earliest days of ATR operations, a pattern began to emerge. Larger, well-capitalized carriers tended to purchase new aircraft directly from the manufacturer, often as launch customers for upgraded variants. After a decade or more of service, as airlines modernized their fleets or shifted strategies, these aircraft would be retired from frontline operations. Instead of heading for the scrapyard, ATRs almost invariably found new operators, sometimes in completely different regions of the world. Leasing companies and brokers facilitated this transition, creating a thriving ecosystem where ATRs changed hands multiple times, yet continued to provide valuable service.

Europe, as ATR's home market, was the first region where this dynamic took root. Airlines in France, Italy, and the United Kingdom introduced ATRs into their fleets in the 1980s and 1990s. As time went on and airlines sought to standardize fleets with newer models, older ATRs were sold or leased to smaller operators in Eastern Europe, Africa, and Asia. This cascading ownership ensured that the aircraft remained in service for far longer than a typical economic lifespan might suggest. Some ATR 42s delivered in the mid-1980s were still flying passenger services well into the 2010s, having passed through three or four different owners.

The economic argument for second-hand ATRs was compelling. A new ATR 72 might cost an airline upwards of $20 million, while a well-maintained used example could be acquired for a fraction of that cost. For small regional carriers operating in developing economies, this difference was decisive. The used aircraft allowed them to expand networks, increase frequencies, or enter new markets without crippling debt or capital outlays. Leasing firms capitalized on this demand by building dedicated ATR portfolios, offering flexible lease terms to operators that could not commit to new aircraft purchases.

The Caribbean and Latin America provided early examples of this second-hand cycle in action. Larger carriers in Europe or North America retired aircraft after years of service, only for those same aircraft to find new lives on island-hopping routes in the Caribbean or short domestic hops in Central America. Airlines such as LIAT and Aeromar often operated ATRs that had previously flown in Europe. Despite their age, these aircraft proved entirely capable of fulfilling demanding schedules across challenging geographies. For the passengers boarding these planes, the age of the aircraft was far less important than the fact that it provided safe, reliable, and affordable travel.

Africa became another major destination for second-hand ATRs. Airlines across the continent often lacked the financial resources to purchase new aircraft, and second-hand turboprops provided the ideal balance between cost and capability. From West Africa to East Africa, ATRs entered service with carriers operating under difficult economic conditions, yet the aircraft managed to thrive. Their ability to handle short, unpaved, or poorly maintained runways made them well suited to the realities of African infrastructure. Leasing companies based in Europe and the Middle East developed strong ties with African operators, creating pipelines through which retired European aircraft were refurbished and redeployed across the continent.

What made the secondary market particularly vibrant was ATR's adaptability to new roles. Beyond conventional passenger service, many used ATRs were converted into freighters. Passenger-to-freighter (P2F) conversions became a significant driver of demand, particularly as e-commerce began to reshape logistics industries worldwide. Companies like FedEx recognized the ATR's potential as a regional freighter, introducing fleets of ATR 42 and ATR 72 freighters into service to handle short-haul cargo operations. Smaller logistics providers across Latin America, Asia, and Africa followed suit, relying on converted ATRs to move goods into secondary markets where larger freighters could not land. This gave a second lease of life to aircraft that might otherwise have been retired.

The economics of conversion further reinforced the value of used ATRs. Converting a passenger aircraft into a freighter was far cheaper than building a new one, and the result was a rugged, fuel-efficient cargo plane that could operate profitably on short routes. Many aircraft transitioned seamlessly from carrying holidaymakers in Europe to delivering parcels in South America or medical supplies in Africa. This adaptability underscored the ATR's core design strengths and helped cement its reputation as a versatile workhorse.

Leasing companies became central players in the second-hand ATR market. Firms such as Nordic Aviation Capital (NAC) and Elix Aviation built extensive ATR portfolios, offering hundreds of aircraft to operators around the world. Their business models relied heavily on the durability and broad applicability of the ATR, allowing them to lease aircraft to airlines in widely different environments. Leasing ensured a continuous flow of ATRs across the globe, reducing downtime between ownership cycles and providing smaller operators with access to aircraft without the burdens of ownership.

In Asia-Pacific, the demand for second-hand ATRs surged during the 2000s and 2010s as regional aviation markets expanded. India's growth was particularly notable, with airlines such as IndiGo and Alliance Air building fleets of ATR 72s to connect smaller cities. While many of these aircraft were acquired new, the expansion created demand for used ATRs to supplement capacity. Similarly, in Indonesia and the Philippines, second-hand ATRs played a major role in expanding connectivity across islands. Smaller start-up carriers often relied on leased or purchased used aircraft to test markets, only upgrading to new aircraft once they had proven demand.

The resale value of ATRs became one of their most attractive features. While many aircraft depreciate quickly, ATRs held their value well because of the continuous demand in secondary markets. This made them appealing to lessors and original operators alike, as resale could recoup a significant portion of the initial investment. For airlines considering new ATR purchases, the knowledge that they could later sell the aircraft into a vibrant secondary market provided an additional layer of financial security.

Maintenance and support were key to sustaining this second-hand ecosystem. ATR itself, along with third-party maintenance providers, offered comprehensive support programs for older aircraft. This ensured that even as aircraft aged, they could continue to meet safety and regulatory standards. Refurbishment programs extended aircraft lifespans, upgrading avionics, interiors, and systems to make older aircraft more appealing to new operators. These programs demonstrated ATR's recognition that its market did not end with new sales but extended into the entire lifecycle of the aircraft.

In some cases, second-hand ATRs even played roles in humanitarian and governmental operations. Non-governmental organizations, charter companies, and government agencies acquired used ATRs to deliver aid, transport personnel, or perform surveillance missions. Their affordability and ruggedness made them suitable for these roles, where budgets were limited but reliability was essential. ATR's entry into these sectors further diversified its footprint and underscored the wide range of opportunities in the secondary market.

The global spread of second-hand ATRs created a unique situation where aircraft built in Toulouse or Naples could spend their operational lives traveling across multiple continents. An ATR 42 might begin service in Europe, move to the Caribbean, and later end its career in Africa. Each stage of its life represented a different type of operator, passenger, and mission, yet the aircraft remained fundamentally the same: a reliable turboprop designed for short-haul efficiency. This mobility reinforced ATR's global brand, as its aircraft became visible in even the most remote corners of the world.

The strength of the second-hand market also shielded ATR from some of the cyclical downturns in aviation. During times when new aircraft orders slowed due to economic recessions or fuel price volatility, demand for second-hand aircraft often remained stable or even increased, as airlines sought cost-effective ways to maintain or expand capacity. Leasing companies in particular benefitted during these downturns, providing airlines with access to affordable ATRs when capital expenditures on new aircraft were not feasible.

By the late 2010s, the secondary market had become such a cornerstone of ATR's identity that it was discussed alongside new aircraft sales in industry analyses. ATR's value proposition extended far beyond Toulouse's production lines; it encompassed a global network of lessors, brokers, conversion firms, and operators who together kept the aircraft in service for decades. Few regional aircraft could boast such resilience.

As the 2020s began, the importance of the second-hand market was only reinforced by the disruptions of the COVID-19 pandemic. Airlines worldwide struggled with collapsing demand, but the ATR's economics and the flexibility of the leasing market enabled many operators to downsize fleets or restructure operations without abandoning regional routes. Used ATRs, with their lower capital costs and efficient performance, became lifelines for airlines seeking to weather the crisis.

In the long view, the second-hand market for ATRs demonstrates one of the company's most remarkable achievements: creating an aircraft not just for one generation of operators but for multiple ones. The ATR was never disposable—it was built to last, and that longevity created a thriving ecosystem where aircraft continued to deliver value long after their first flights. The story of ATR cannot be told without recognizing the thousands of flights flown by used aircraft, serving passengers who may never have known they were stepping aboard machines with decades of history behind them.

In this enduring market, the ATR became more than an aircraft. It became a renewable asset, circulating across continents and adapting to new challenges. Its journey through the second-hand market reflects the resilience of regional aviation itself, where necessity, geography, and economics intersect to keep aircraft in the sky. And in that intersection, the ATR proved once again why it stood apart: not just as a product of European ingenuity, but as a global workhorse whose value multiplied with every new chapter in its operational life.

Chapter 15: Freighter Conversions and Cargo Potential

When ATR was conceived in the early 1980s, its focus was firmly on carrying passengers across short-haul routes that jets could not serve economically. The ATR 42 and later the ATR 72 were designed to shuttle commuters, business travelers, and leisure passengers between regional centers, island communities, and secondary airports. Yet as the years unfolded, another chapter of ATR's story emerged—one that expanded its relevance far beyond passenger travel. The ATR's transformation from a passenger transport to a freighter became one of the most important dimensions of its enduring success, proving that the turboprop could adapt not only across decades but across industries.

The cargo potential of ATRs was not immediately obvious in the 1980s. At the time, dedicated freighter turboprops were limited in scope, with many cargo operators relying on aging piston-engine aircraft like the Douglas DC-3, Convair 580, or Fairchild Metros. These older aircraft were reliable but increasingly inefficient, difficult to maintain, and expensive to operate as they aged. Jet freighters, while offering greater capacity and speed, were unsuited to short, thin routes with small loads. The gap between these extremes left an opportunity that ATR would come to fill, although not deliberately at first.

The initial wave of ATRs that entered service in the mid-1980s and 1990s were exclusively configured for passengers. However, as some of these aircraft aged and cycled out of frontline airline fleets, operators began to explore new uses. The basic qualities of the ATR—fuel efficiency, ruggedness, short takeoff and landing ability, and relatively low maintenance costs—made them ideal candidates for conversion into cargo aircraft. By removing passenger fittings and reinforcing the cabin for freight, ATRs could be repurposed to carry everything from parcels and perishables to industrial parts and humanitarian supplies.

It was not long before major logistics companies recognized the opportunity. FedEx, one of the largest integrated cargo carriers in the world, was among the first to embrace ATRs as regional freighters. The company had long relied on smaller feeder aircraft to distribute packages to and from its larger hubs, but by the early 2000s it was clear that a new generation of efficient turboprops would be needed. The ATR 42 and ATR 72 were a natural fit. Their combination of fuel economy, payload capability, and ability to land on short runways made them perfect for connecting smaller markets to FedEx's global network. FedEx's decision to order and operate fleets of ATR freighters gave an enormous boost to ATR's credibility in the cargo sector.

The relationship with FedEx also marked a turning point in ATR's strategy. Recognizing the growing demand for dedicated freighters, ATR moved beyond ad-hoc passenger-to-freighter (P2F) conversions and began offering factory-built freighter versions. These models, known as the ATR 42F and ATR 72F, were designed from the outset as cargo carriers, with reinforced floors, large cargo doors, and optimized interiors for freight operations. The introduction of factory freighters opened a new chapter for ATR, one where the company was not only competing for airline contracts but also actively shaping regional cargo aviation.

The ATR freighter variants offered several advantages over improvised conversions. The installation of a large forward cargo door, for example, made it far easier to load and unload pallets or containers. Reinforced floors allowed for higher-density freight, ensuring the aircraft could handle everything from mail bags to heavy machinery. The absence of passenger fittings reduced weight and maintenance complexity, while systems were optimized for cargo operations, including lighting and restraint systems designed specifically for freight. These factory-built freighters gave operators a plug-and-play solution that was immediately profitable and efficient.

Parallel to factory production, the aftermarket conversion industry thrived. Many passenger ATRs reaching the end of their airline careers were purchased by leasing companies or brokers and converted into freighters. Specialized firms offered standardized conversion kits that included structural reinforcements, the installation of cargo doors, and certification for freight operations. These conversions allowed aircraft that might otherwise have been retired to extend their service lives by another decade or more. For smaller operators who could not afford new factory freighters, conversions provided a cost-effective entry point into cargo operations.

The rise of e-commerce in the 21st century gave the ATR freighter market a powerful tailwind. Companies like Amazon, Alibaba, and Mercado Libre created unprecedented demand for fast, flexible logistics networks that extended beyond major metropolitan centers. Consumers in smaller cities and rural areas began to expect next-day or even same-day deliveries, forcing logistics companies to develop new ways to serve regional markets. The ATR, with its ability to operate into secondary airports with short runways, became an indispensable link in these networks. It could move packages quickly and efficiently between hubs and outlying communities, ensuring that e-commerce giants could deliver on their promises of speed and reliability.

Geography also played a role in ATR's cargo potential. Island nations and archipelagos, such as Indonesia and the Philippines, required aircraft capable of linking dozens or hundreds of small airports. Cargo flows in these markets were often modest in scale but critical in importance, ranging from essential goods and food supplies to pharmaceuticals and electronics. Jets were simply too large and uneconomical for these missions, but ATR freighters were perfectly sized. They could carry enough cargo to make operations profitable while maintaining the flexibility to land on shorter runways in challenging terrain.

In Africa, ATR freighters became lifelines for communities far from major urban centers. With poor ground infrastructure and vast distances, air cargo often provided the only reliable way to transport goods across countries. ATR freighters carried medical supplies to remote clinics, delivered agricultural products to markets, and transported spare parts to mining operations. Their ability to fly into airstrips with minimal facilities gave them a competitive edge over larger freighters, which were restricted to major airports. For humanitarian organizations, ATR freighters also became vital tools, enabling rapid response during crises such as famines, natural disasters, or disease outbreaks.

Latin America mirrored this trend, with ATR freighters taking on crucial roles in countries like Brazil, Colombia, and Mexico. Mountainous terrain and vast rural areas created unique logistical challenges that could only be solved by small, efficient freighters. Converted ATRs, many sourced from European or North American airlines, became the backbone of regional cargo operations. They carried everything from flowers and coffee beans to pharmaceuticals and industrial equipment, weaving together economies that might otherwise have remained disconnected.

One of the strengths of ATR freighters lay in their operating economics. Turboprops were inherently more fuel-efficient than regional jets, especially on short routes. Their ability to fly sectors of 200 to 400 kilometers at lower costs gave them a decisive edge in regional cargo markets. Operators often noted that an ATR freighter could operate profitably with relatively low payloads, a crucial advantage in markets where cargo volumes fluctuated or remained limited. This efficiency kept ATR freighters flying even during downturns, when larger freighters were often grounded due to insufficient demand.

Another factor in ATR's cargo success was its partnership with leasing companies. Firms like Nordic Aviation Capital not only leased passenger ATRs but also developed large portfolios of converted freighters. These lessors offered flexible arrangements that allowed operators to scale up or down based on market conditions. For many start-up cargo airlines, leasing a converted ATR was the gateway into the industry, providing access to aircraft without requiring enormous upfront investment. The availability of such arrangements fueled further growth in the ATR freighter market.

The ATR freighter story is also one of continuous technical evolution. ATR introduced improved freighter versions with better avionics, higher payload capacities, and optimized cargo handling systems. The ATR 72-600F, for example, became a flagship model in the freighter lineup. Designed from the ground up for cargo operations, it included features such as a reinforced fuselage, larger cargo door, and systems tailored for freight. Customers praised its ability to carry up to 9 tonnes of cargo efficiently across short distances, making it one of the most capable regional freighters on the market.

Environmental considerations also played into ATR's growing role in the cargo market. As the aviation industry faced pressure to reduce emissions, ATR freighters provided a relatively green alternative. Their lower fuel burn and reduced carbon output made them attractive to operators seeking to demonstrate sustainability credentials. For logistics companies increasingly under scrutiny for their environmental impact, deploying ATR freighters became a way to balance economic efficiency with ecological responsibility.

The cultural perception of ATR freighters also deserves attention. While passenger ATRs were often seen as modest, utilitarian aircraft compared to glamorous jets, the freighter versions earned admiration for their reliability and indispensability. Within the cargo sector, they became known as workhorses, capable of handling demanding schedules in challenging conditions. Pilots and operators frequently noted that ATR freighters were forgiving to fly, straightforward to maintain, and versatile enough to adapt to a wide variety of missions. This reputation further strengthened their position in the global cargo market.

Perhaps the most telling measure of ATR's success in cargo is the simple fact that many of its aircraft, after decades of carrying passengers, found renewed life carrying freight. Instead of being scrapped, these aircraft were given new missions, extending their relevance and economic value. The cycle of passenger service followed by cargo conversion became a defining feature of the ATR lifecycle. It ensured that even as new aircraft rolled off production lines in Toulouse, older ones continued to deliver value in entirely different ways.

The long-term significance of ATR's freighter conversions and factory-built freighters cannot be overstated. They allowed the company to diversify beyond the passenger airline market, reducing vulnerability to shifts in tourism or business travel. Cargo demand, while subject to cycles, was less volatile and often countercyclical to passenger traffic, providing stability during downturns. By tapping into this market, ATR not only increased aircraft sales but also enhanced its resilience as a manufacturer.

By the 2020s, the sight of ATR freighters operating in FedEx colors, carrying parcels across Europe in DHL service, or delivering goods across remote parts of Asia and Africa had become commonplace. They were no longer a niche product but an integral part of global logistics. In a world increasingly dependent on fast, flexible delivery systems, ATR freighters occupied a space no other aircraft could fill so effectively.

In retrospect, the transformation of ATR into a cargo player reflects the company's broader identity: adaptive, resilient, and indispensable. From carrying commuters across European regional routes to delivering e-commerce parcels in Asia and humanitarian supplies in Africa, ATR proved that its aircraft were not bound to a single role. They could evolve, finding new relevance as the aviation landscape changed. The freighter story, therefore, is not just about cargo; it is about ATR's capacity to reinvent itself while staying true to its core design principles.

As global trade and e-commerce continue to expand, the demand for efficient regional freighters shows no sign of abating. ATR's ability to deliver solutions across both the passenger and cargo sectors ensures that its aircraft will remain central to aviation networks worldwide. Whether carrying people or packages, fresh deliveries or life-saving medicines, ATR aircraft continue to connect communities in ways that larger aircraft simply cannot. And in doing so, they affirm a legacy not only of endurance but of adaptability—the hallmark of a company that found in cargo yet another way to stay indispensable to global aviation.

Chapter 16: Inside the Cabin – Passenger Experience

For most of its life, ATR has been judged not only by its performance and operating economics but also by the experience it offered inside the cabin. Though the ATR was designed as a functional regional aircraft, the passenger's perspective always mattered. Airlines knew that travelers compared turboprops to jets, often unfavorably, associating propellers with noise, vibration, and older aircraft. Overcoming that stigma required careful attention to cabin design, noise reduction, and comfort. As the ATR family evolved, so too did its interiors, reflecting both technological advances and shifting expectations among passengers. The story of ATR's cabin is therefore as central to its success as its engines or wings, for it speaks directly to how airlines sold the turboprop to the traveling public.

When the ATR 42 entered service in the mid-1980s, regional aviation was a far cry from the standards familiar today. Short-haul flights were often marketed as no-frills services. Cabins were compact, seats narrow, and amenities sparse. Airlines assumed that passengers boarding a 45-minute or one-hour turboprop hop would prioritize schedule and convenience over comfort. ATR's early cabins reflected this utilitarian approach. The 2-2 seating configuration maximized capacity within the narrow fuselage, offering a typical seat pitch of 30 to 32 inches. Overhead bins were small, designed for briefcases or coats rather than wheeled carry-ons. Lighting was basic, and air circulation systems did their job but without finesse.

Noise, however, was the defining feature of early ATR cabins. The twin turboprops, mounted close to the fuselage, generated a constant hum and vibration that filled the interior. Compared to jets, where engines were typically mounted further aft or on the wings away from the fuselage, turboprops subjected passengers to a more intrusive acoustic environment. For some travelers, this became a deterrent, reinforcing the perception of turboprops as outdated or uncomfortable. Airlines operating ATRs were aware of this challenge, and ATR itself understood that cabin noise would have to be addressed if the aircraft was to compete for passenger loyalty.

Despite these limitations, early ATR cabins were not without their merits. The relatively low cabin altitude, maintained by pressurization suitable for short flights, made for a comfortable breathing environment compared to smaller commuter aircraft that were unpressurized. The wide windows of the ATR allowed for generous natural light, a feature passengers appreciated, particularly on scenic flights over islands or mountains. The simple cabin layout also made boarding and deplaning efficient, an important consideration on routes where quick turnarounds were critical.

By the 1990s, however, passenger expectations had begun to rise. The proliferation of regional jets, particularly Bombardier's CRJ and Embraer's ERJ families, introduced new benchmarks for comfort on short-haul routes. Airlines realized that to persuade travelers to choose turboprops over jets, the passenger experience would have to improve.

ATR responded with a series of upgrades aimed at noise reduction, interior refinement, and overall cabin ambiance.

Noise abatement became a central focus. ATR engineers worked extensively on propeller design, blade aerodynamics, and cabin insulation. The adoption of six-bladed propellers on later ATR models significantly reduced noise and vibration levels inside the cabin. Advanced materials in the insulation layers, combined with improved sealing around windows and doors, further lessened the intrusive hum of the engines. While no turboprop could be as quiet as a regional jet, the difference was enough to change perceptions. Passengers who once dreaded the "buzz" of turboprop travel began to remark on quieter, more comfortable rides, particularly on the ATR 72 series.

Airlines, too, began to see the cabin as a space to differentiate their service. Some operators chose to configure ATRs with fewer seats to provide more legroom, particularly on routes targeting business travelers. Others installed leather seating, upgraded lighting systems, and improved galleys to support catering. The ATR's flexible cabin design allowed for such customization, giving airlines the ability to match interiors to their market strategy. For carriers in island nations like Air Tahiti or Caribbean Airlines, cabins were often styled with bright colors and local motifs to create a welcoming atmosphere, turning the ATR into part of the holiday experience.

As technology advanced, ATR introduced new cabin concepts under its "Armonia" brand, unveiled in the late 2000s. Armonia cabins, designed in collaboration with Italian design house Giugiaro, represented a leap forward in passenger experience. They featured reshaped overhead bins that increased storage capacity for modern carry-on luggage, improved LED lighting systems that created a brighter and more spacious feel, and ergonomic seating that enhanced comfort on short flights. The streamlined design not only looked more modern but also reduced maintenance complexity, a benefit to operators.

The Armonia cabin also addressed one of the subtler challenges of regional travel: the psychological impact of space. Narrow fuselages can make cabins feel cramped, but by refining seat contours, redesigning sidewalls, and incorporating brighter finishes, ATR created an impression of greater openness. Passengers accustomed to squeezing bags under seats or juggling personal items found the larger bins a welcome relief, while the lighting improved mood and reduced fatigue. For many, the Armonia cabins closed the gap between turboprops and jets in terms of perceived comfort.

Noise reduction remained a theme in the ATR 600 series, which incorporated advanced vibration-dampening systems and further refinements to propeller aerodynamics. Airlines began to market ATR flights not as compromises but as competitive choices, emphasizing the comfort of the new interiors. Some operators even positioned ATR cabins as boutique experiences, highlighting panoramic views from large windows and promoting the relaxed atmosphere of slower, lower-altitude flight. In tourist markets, this approach resonated strongly, turning what was once a liability into a selling point.

Another dimension of cabin experience was accessibility and inclusivity. As regulations evolved, ATR cabins were adapted to better serve passengers with reduced mobility. Wider aisles, improved lavatories, and redesigned seating areas reflected a growing emphasis on universal design. Airlines recognized that serving all passengers comfortably was not just a regulatory requirement but also a business advantage, expanding their market reach and improving customer satisfaction.

The versatility of ATR cabins also extended beyond passenger comfort. Many operators used quick-change configurations, allowing aircraft to shift from passenger to cargo layouts in a matter of hours. This flexibility was particularly useful for airlines serving regions with fluctuating demand, where a morning passenger flight could be followed by an evening cargo service. Such adaptability further underscored ATR's role as a practical and versatile aircraft family.

Cultural and regional tailoring played a significant role in how ATR cabins were presented. In Southeast Asia, where flights often connected remote islands, ATR cabins were designed for high-density layouts to maximize capacity on routes with strong demand but limited runway length. In contrast, European regional airlines emphasized business-friendly layouts, with fewer seats, more legroom, and premium finishes. African operators often configured cabins for durability and ease of cleaning, recognizing the rugged conditions under which aircraft operated. Each adaptation reinforced the ATR's ability to serve diverse markets without losing sight of passenger experience.

The psychological perception of turboprops also shifted gradually as cabins improved. Where once travelers associated propellers with inconvenience or discomfort, modern ATR cabins helped reshape the narrative. Airlines marketed the aircraft not as outdated but as environmentally friendly, efficient, and modern. Passengers flying on ATR 600 series aircraft increasingly reported positive experiences, noting that the difference between turboprops and regional jets was far smaller than expected. This change in perception was critical, ensuring that ATR remained competitive in a market where passenger satisfaction could make or break route viability.

In recent years, sustainability has become another layer of the passenger experience. Travelers concerned about environmental impact have been more receptive to flying on ATRs when airlines emphasized the aircraft's fuel efficiency and lower emissions. Cabin messaging, in-flight literature, and even design motifs began to incorporate green themes, subtly aligning the passenger experience with broader narratives about responsible travel. In this way, the cabin became not just a space of comfort but also a space of communication, reinforcing the airline's values and ATR's positioning.

The ATR's cabin story is therefore one of continuous refinement. From the noisy, utilitarian interiors of the 1980s to the modern, thoughtfully designed Armonia cabins of the

600 series, the evolution reflects both technological progress and a deeper understanding of passenger psychology. Airlines and ATR together recognized that even on short flights, comfort mattered, and perception was everything. By improving noise control, upgrading seating and storage, and allowing operators to tailor interiors to local markets, ATR turned its cabins from potential weaknesses into strengths.

As aviation looks toward the future, the cabin will remain central to the ATR experience. With passengers demanding ever greater comfort, connectivity, and sustainability, ATR continues to explore new cabin innovations, from improved materials to digital in-flight services. What began as a functional commuter aircraft interior has become a platform for innovation, branding, and passenger satisfaction. And in that journey, the ATR has proven that even the smallest details inside the cabin can shape the destiny of an aircraft family across generations.

Chapter 17: Manufacturing and Supply Chain

The ATR story cannot be told without a close look at the industrial backbone that sustained it. Unlike many aircraft programs where design, production, and final assembly are concentrated in a single country, ATR emerged from a uniquely European collaboration that spread its supply chain across borders. From the very beginning, the joint venture between France's Aérospatiale and Italy's Aeritalia meant that no single nation could claim ownership of the aircraft in entirety. Instead, production responsibilities were divided, with Toulouse serving as the final assembly site but components flowing in from Italy and numerous other European partners. This arrangement reflected both political necessity and industrial strategy. It also gave ATR an international character, embedding in its DNA a reliance on multinational coordination, which would remain central to its operations for decades.

The foundations of this supply chain were laid in the early 1980s. France took the lead in establishing Toulouse as the site for final assembly, leveraging its existing infrastructure and experience in aircraft production. Aeritalia, meanwhile, was entrusted with critical elements of the structure, including major fuselage sections and tail assemblies. This division of labor ensured that both nations had a stake in the program's success, an arrangement that made the ATR project politically palatable in Paris and Rome. The European aerospace industry was then in a period of consolidation, and joint projects like ATR served as a proving ground for cooperative manufacturing models that would later become common across Airbus programs.

The ATR 42, the program's first aircraft, set the tone for this distributed production system. Wings were manufactured in France, fuselage sections in Italy, and other key components in various subcontractor facilities across Europe. These parts converged in Toulouse, where they were joined together, systems were installed, interiors were fitted, and flight testing was conducted. From the outside, this may have seemed a complex and perhaps unwieldy arrangement, but it offered several advantages. First, it allowed each partner nation to preserve industrial jobs, spreading the economic benefits of the program. Second, it tapped into existing expertise: Aeritalia had extensive experience with fuselage production, while Aérospatiale excelled in wing design and final assembly. The result was a supply chain that balanced politics with efficiency.

Over the years, as ATR introduced the ATR 72 and later the 600 series, the supply chain expanded and evolved. What remained constant, however, was the central role of Toulouse. Every ATR aircraft, regardless of model, would eventually find its way to southwestern France for final assembly. This site became not just a manufacturing hub but also a symbol of ATR's identity. For customers, Toulouse was where the aircraft came to life, where painted tail fins representing airlines from across the world lined up on the tarmac awaiting delivery.

Inside the Toulouse facility, production was organized around a modular philosophy. Large pre-fabricated sections arrived by truck or air transport and were joined on the assembly line. This modularity reduced the complexity of final assembly and shortened production timelines. It also meant that improvements in one part of the supply chain could be implemented without disrupting the entire system. For example, when new materials or design enhancements were introduced in fuselage sections, they could be integrated seamlessly into the flow toward Toulouse. This flexibility proved vital in maintaining efficiency as the aircraft family evolved.

The European supply network that sustained ATR was both a strength and a challenge. On one hand, it anchored the program in multiple industrial bases, ensuring political support. On the other hand, it required meticulous coordination to manage logistics, quality standards, and timelines. A delay in fuselage delivery from Italy, for example, could hold up assembly in Toulouse. ATR therefore invested heavily in systems to track and synchronize production flows. As the company matured, it became adept at balancing these demands, turning what could have been a vulnerability into a finely tuned orchestration of international manufacturing.

Beyond Europe, ATR also relied on a web of global suppliers. Avionics systems, engines, and interior fittings often came from specialized companies located outside the Franco-Italian partnership. Pratt & Whitney Canada supplied the PW100 family of engines, a cornerstone of ATR performance. Avionics systems came from firms such as Thales and Collins, reflecting the global nature of aerospace sourcing. Cabin interiors were often sourced from a variety of manufacturers, with airlines sometimes specifying their own suppliers for seats, galleys, or inflight entertainment systems. This global integration required ATR to maintain strong relationships with suppliers across continents, balancing cost, quality, and delivery schedules.

The manufacturing philosophy behind ATR also emphasized continuous refinement rather than dramatic reinvention. Instead of launching entirely new aircraft every decade, ATR preferred to upgrade existing models with incremental improvements. This strategy had direct implications for the supply chain. Rather than retooling entire factories, suppliers could adapt their production processes to accommodate new avionics, improved materials, or updated systems. For instance, when ATR introduced the Armonia cabin, interior suppliers adjusted their designs and tooling to produce the new seats, bins, and lighting, but the fundamental fuselage structure remained the same. This incremental approach allowed ATR to keep costs under control while steadily improving the product.

At the heart of ATR's production process was the principle of lean manufacturing. The company embraced efficiency, minimizing waste and optimizing workflows to reduce costs. Given that ATR's competitive edge lay partly in affordability—both for purchase and operation—keeping production expenses under control was vital. Toulouse became a showcase for streamlined assembly, where a relatively small workforce could produce dozens of aircraft each year. The simplicity of the ATR's systems compared to jets also meant that assembly lines could move quickly, delivering aircraft on schedule to customers worldwide.

The importance of Toulouse extended beyond the factory floor. The city became a focal point for customer engagement, training, and delivery ceremonies. Airlines frequently sent teams to oversee their aircraft's final stages of production, inspect interiors, and conduct acceptance flights. Toulouse thus became a global meeting ground for ATR customers, suppliers, and employees, reinforcing the company's identity as a hub of regional aviation.

As demand for ATRs grew, particularly in Asia-Pacific and Latin America, the supply chain faced new pressures. Production rates had to increase to meet orders, and suppliers were pushed to scale up their output without sacrificing quality. ATR worked closely with its partners to expand capacity, sometimes bringing in new subcontractors to support growing demand. Maintaining consistency across this expanding network was not always easy, but ATR's reputation for reliability meant that quality control was non-negotiable. Rigorous inspections, certification processes, and supplier audits ensured that each aircraft met exacting standards before joining the assembly line.

The globalization of ATR's supply chain also raised questions about risk management. Natural disasters, political instability, or economic disruptions in supplier countries had the potential to ripple through the system. To mitigate these risks, ATR developed contingency plans and diversified sourcing where possible. The importance of resilience became particularly evident in times of crisis, such as the

2008 financial downturn or the COVID-19 pandemic, when supply chains worldwide were disrupted. ATR's ability to weather these challenges owed much to its decades of experience in managing complexity and its relatively modest production volumes compared to large jet manufacturers.

The Toulouse site itself evolved over time, incorporating new technologies and expanding facilities to handle increased demand. Computer-aided design (CAD) and digital production planning streamlined workflows, reducing errors and optimizing efficiency. Robotics and automation were introduced selectively, particularly in repetitive tasks such as drilling or fastening, while skilled workers continued to play a central role in assembly. The balance between automation and craftsmanship reflected the scale of ATR production: too small to justify full automation but large enough to benefit from targeted technological support.

The supply chain also carried symbolic importance for European industrial cooperation. At a time when debates about sovereignty and integration often made headlines, ATR stood as a tangible example of successful cross-border collaboration. The smooth functioning of its supply chain demonstrated that shared goals and mutual benefit could overcome national rivalries. This symbolism was not lost on policymakers, who often cited ATR as a model for future European industrial projects.

Environmental considerations gradually became part of the supply chain conversation as well. ATR and its partners began exploring more sustainable manufacturing practices, from reducing waste in production to sourcing materials with lower environmental footprints. Toulouse, in particular, became a testbed for greener manufacturing processes, aligning with the broader aviation industry's push toward sustainability. These initiatives were not only about corporate responsibility but also about strengthening ATR's brand as an environmentally friendly alternative in regional aviation.

The supply chain extended into the aftermarket too. Supporting hundreds of ATR aircraft worldwide required a robust system for spare parts, maintenance, and training. Toulouse played a role here as well, housing logistics centers that dispatched components to operators around the globe. Regional support hubs in Asia, the Americas, and Africa complemented this system, ensuring that airlines could keep their ATR fleets flying with minimal downtime. The integration of manufacturing and aftermarket support created a virtuous cycle, reinforcing ATR's relationship with customers long after delivery.

Looking at ATR's manufacturing and supply chain, one is struck by its adaptability. What began as a politically driven division of labor between France and Italy grew into a finely balanced global network capable of delivering reliable aircraft for decades. The supply chain's success lay not in its simplicity but in its complexity managed well. It was a living system, evolving with each new aircraft variant, each technological upgrade, and each shift in market demand.

Ultimately, ATR's supply chain was more than just a logistical necessity; it was part of the company's identity. It embodied the spirit of European cooperation, the pragmatism of lean manufacturing, and the resilience needed to navigate a volatile global industry. Toulouse may have been the heart where ATR aircraft came together, but the lifeblood flowed in from every corner of Europe and beyond. Each ATR delivered to airlines carried with it not just wings and fuselages, but also the story of thousands of skilled hands across continents working in harmony. That story, written in rivets, composites, and systems, ensured that ATR remained not just a product of its partners but a symbol of enduring international collaboration in aviation.

Chapter 18: Partnerships with Regional Airlines

ATR's story is not just the history of a company or an aircraft type—it is, at its core, the history of partnerships. From the very beginning, ATR's survival depended on building close relationships with the world's regional airlines, many of which lacked the resources, visibility, or bargaining power of larger national carriers. These partnerships went far beyond simple aircraft sales. They encompassed training, financing, technical support, and operational integration, creating bonds that allowed smaller airlines to thrive and, in turn, ensured ATR's aircraft were used to their fullest potential. To understand ATR's global legacy, one must look not only at Toulouse or Naples but at the dozens of regional airports scattered across islands, mountain valleys, and secondary cities where ATR aircraft became synonymous with connectivity.

The ATR 42, launched in 1985, set the pattern for these partnerships. Unlike jets of the time, which were typically purchased by larger airlines with long-haul ambitions, the ATR was aimed at carriers operating short routes, often with limited infrastructure. Many of these airlines flew aging fleets of smaller turboprops like the Fokker F27, Handley Page Herald, or various Japanese and Soviet types. For them, acquiring a new ATR represented a leap in reliability, efficiency, and passenger comfort. ATR recognized early that these operators would need more than an aircraft—they would need a package of support to ensure they could sustain operations in competitive markets.

One of ATR's early strategies was to establish a strong customer support framework. This involved training pilots, mechanics, and ground crew, often from airlines that had limited prior exposure to Western-built aircraft. Toulouse became a hub for training programs, but ATR also sent teams abroad to work alongside airline staff in their home countries. These relationships created a sense of partnership rather than mere vendor-client interaction. Airlines came to view ATR not simply as a manufacturer but as a collaborator invested in their success.

Airlines like Air Littoral in France, Finnaviation in Finland, and Avanti Air in Germany were among the early adopters, each finding in the ATR 42 a tool perfectly suited to their networks. As word spread of the aircraft's reliability and low fuel burn, interest grew among regional carriers worldwide. In many cases, ATR made sales by proving that its aircraft could transform the economics of regional air travel. Demonstration tours showcased not just performance but also the practicality of operating from short runways, gravel strips, or airports in hot and high conditions. These demos often included airline executives, government officials, and even local media, reinforcing the idea that an ATR purchase was an investment in regional development.

In the Asia-Pacific, partnerships reached an entirely new scale. Airlines in Indonesia, the Philippines, and later India discovered that the ATR was tailor-made for their geographic realities. The Philippines, an archipelago of more than 7,000 islands, required a reliable short-haul aircraft capable of frequent takeoffs and landings on relatively short runways.

Cebu Pacific and other carriers built large ATR fleets precisely because the aircraft matched the contours of their market. ATR, for its part, cultivated these relationships by offering tailored support, including on-site training centers and spare parts hubs. These steps ensured that the airlines could maximize utilization and minimize downtime—critical factors in markets where even a single grounded aircraft could disrupt an entire network.

In Indonesia, Lion Air's regional arm, Wings Air, became one of ATR's largest customers. At its peak, Wings Air operated more than 70 ATRs, weaving them into a dense network that connected secondary cities and smaller communities beyond the reach of Boeing and Airbus jets. For ATR, this was not just a sale; it was a strategic partnership that proved the viability of large turboprop fleets in modern aviation. ATR staff worked closely with Wings Air to align aircraft deliveries with network expansion, fine-tune maintenance schedules for tropical conditions, and train hundreds of local pilots. The success of this partnership demonstrated ATR's philosophy: the aircraft was only as valuable as the ecosystem that supported it.

Similar stories played out in Latin America. In Colombia, Avianca's regional subsidiaries adopted ATRs to connect mountainous cities and towns that were otherwise difficult to reach. The aircraft's ability to operate efficiently in high-altitude conditions made it indispensable in the Andes. In Brazil, Azul Brazilian Airlines integrated ATRs into its network to link smaller cities across a vast territory. Here again, ATR worked hand-in-hand with the airline to ensure that the aircraft met the demands of frequent, short-haul operations. For Azul, ATRs were not a marginal fleet addition but a cornerstone of its business model.

In Africa, the partnership model often extended into nation-building. Many African carriers lacked resources for large fleets of jets, but ATR provided a cost-effective solution that made national connectivity feasible. Airlines like Air Senegal, Air Burkina, and Precision Air in Tanzania built their networks around ATRs, sometimes with the support of government programs or international development funding. ATR played a diplomatic role in these contexts, often working with financial institutions to secure lease deals or government-backed loans. These arrangements helped establish ATR not only as a manufacturer but also as a facilitator of growth for emerging carriers.

One striking example came from Air Tahiti in French Polynesia. Spread across vast stretches of the Pacific, the airline required dependable short-haul aircraft capable of linking dozens of small islands. ATR became the backbone of its fleet, with the turboprops flying some of the most scenic yet demanding routes in the world. ATR worked with Air Tahiti to develop unique cabin layouts optimized for tourist traffic, highlighting the aircraft's adaptability to different market needs. For passengers, ATR became synonymous with the very experience of traveling across Polynesia, blending seamlessly into the identity of the airline and the region.

These partnerships were not always smooth. The U.S. market, for instance, proved a tougher challenge. Many

American regional airlines were tied closely to major carriers through code-sharing agreements, and their fleet decisions were influenced by the preferences of larger partners. Jets often won favor, particularly in the 1990s and 2000s, when passenger perceptions leaned toward speed and modernity. ATR did establish a presence through operators like American Eagle and Continental Express, but the partnerships lacked the depth and longevity seen elsewhere. Regulatory hurdles, such as icing certification requirements, also created friction. Still, ATR learned valuable lessons from these experiences, refining its approach to customer engagement and technical support.

Another dimension of ATR's partnership philosophy was flexibility in financing. Many regional airlines operated on thin margins, making large upfront capital expenditures difficult. ATR worked closely with leasing companies to facilitate aircraft access, ensuring that even small carriers could acquire modern turboprops. By the late 1990s and 2000s, a robust leasing market had emerged for ATRs, further lowering barriers to entry. This arrangement benefited both ATR and its airline customers, fostering long-term relationships that often led to repeat orders.

The evolution of the ATR 72 provided further opportunities for partnership. With its greater seating capacity, the ATR 72 opened new possibilities for airlines seeking to expand without transitioning to jets. Carriers like Bangkok Airways in Thailand and Binter Canarias in Spain's Canary Islands embraced the ATR 72 as the perfect balance between capacity and efficiency. These airlines worked closely with

ATR to customize interiors, schedules, and support systems that maximized the aircraft's value. Over time, the ATR 72 became the most visible face of the brand, cementing partnerships across continents.

An important part of these relationships was ATR's willingness to listen. Feedback from regional airlines shaped many of the incremental upgrades introduced over the years. Airlines requested quieter cabins, more modern avionics, and better cargo capacity—and ATR responded. The introduction of the ATR 600 series was the culmination of years of dialogue with operators. By integrating glass cockpits, more comfortable interiors, and improved performance, ATR reinforced the message that it was evolving alongside its partners.

Even in times of crisis, ATR's partnerships proved resilient. During the global financial downturn of 2008 and the COVID-19 pandemic of 2020, regional airlines faced existential challenges. ATR worked to support operators through flexible maintenance programs, deferred payments, and continued training. The nature of turboprop operations—focused on short routes and secondary markets—often made ATR-equipped airlines more adaptable during downturns. For example, during COVID-19, some ATR operators quickly pivoted to cargo or repatriation flights, with ATR assisting in the necessary technical adjustments.

The depth of ATR's airline partnerships can be seen in the loyalty of certain carriers. Binter Canarias, for example, has operated ATRs continuously since the 1980s, becoming one of the manufacturer's flagship customers. Similarly,

Caribbean airlines such as LIAT and Caribbean Airlines built decades-long relationships with ATR, to the point where the aircraft became inseparable from the identity of regional aviation in the islands. These examples underscore the long-term trust that ATR cultivated through consistent support, adaptability, and shared growth.

Ultimately, ATR's partnerships with regional airlines are what gave meaning to its aircraft. Unlike the glamour associated with widebody jets or the prestige of flag carriers, ATR's story is one of quiet, essential connectivity. It is about aircraft landing in places far removed from global aviation hubs, carrying passengers who may have no other reliable transport option. For these communities, the airline and the aircraft are lifelines, and ATR's success lies in recognizing and supporting that reality.

The relationships forged between ATR and its airline partners were not one-sided transactions; they were symbiotic. Regional carriers gained access to dependable aircraft, tailored support, and global expertise. ATR, in return, gained a global network of loyal operators who proved that turboprops could remain relevant in a jet-driven age. The result was a business model built not on scale alone but on intimacy—a manufacturer that understood the unique challenges of small airlines and embraced them as opportunities.

As ATR moved further into the 21st century, this partnership-driven philosophy remained central. Whether in the dense island networks of Southeast Asia, the rugged highlands of South America, or the vast deserts and savannahs of Africa,

ATR aircraft continued to symbolize collaboration between a European manufacturer and airlines rooted in local contexts. In many ways, these partnerships were the company's most enduring achievement: proof that global aviation could be shaped not only by the giants of the sky but also by the quiet workhorses that carried people to the places where life unfolded every day.

Chapter 19: Competition and Consolidation

From the outset of its creation in the early 1980s, ATR was aware that it was not entering a vacuum. Regional aviation was already populated by established names, from Fokker in the Netherlands to de Havilland Canada and its Dash 7 and Dash 8 turboprops. Over the following decades, ATR's fortunes would be inseparably tied to how it competed against these rivals and, later, how it adapted to an industry in which many of those rivals disappeared through consolidation or exited the market altogether. The story of ATR's resilience is, in many ways, the story of how one small Franco-Italian venture managed to endure while others faltered in the relentless churn of global aviation economics.

In the 1980s, ATR's most immediate competitor was the de Havilland Canada Dash 8. The Dash 8, first flown in 1983, offered a distinctly North American approach to regional aviation. Where the ATR 42 was designed with European secondary airports in mind—short fields, smaller runways, lower passenger volumes—the Dash 8 emphasized performance in hot and high conditions and rugged environments. Its Canadian heritage was apparent in its ability to operate in extreme weather, from Arctic cold to tropical heat, with robust landing gear and systems designed to withstand harsh conditions. For airlines, the Dash 8 represented a proven, reliable choice backed by the long history of de Havilland's earlier turboprops, including the famous Twin Otter and Dash 7.

ATR, by contrast, was a newcomer. To win orders, it had to prove that its aircraft were not only cheaper to operate but also modern in design. The ATR 42 offered lower fuel burn per seat compared to the Dash 8's early versions, and ATR marketed this efficiency aggressively. Airlines operating short routes where runway length and fuel economy mattered more than extreme-weather ruggedness found the ATR compelling. This set the stage for decades of head-to-head rivalry, with ATR and the Dash 8 family becoming the two dominant turboprop lines worldwide.

The rivalry intensified with the introduction of larger models. In 1988, ATR launched the ATR 72, extending seating capacity beyond 70 passengers. De Havilland responded by stretching the Dash 8 into the 300 and later 400 series, the latter capable of seating up to 90 passengers. The Dash 8-400, later branded as the Q400, became the closest direct competitor to ATR's largest model. Its higher cruise speed, closer to that of regional jets, was its defining advantage. Bombardier, which had acquired de Havilland Canada in 1992, marketed the Q400 as a "jet replacement turboprop," targeting airlines that wanted the economics of a turboprop without sacrificing too much on speed.

For ATR, this was both a challenge and an opportunity. The ATR 72 could not match the Dash 8-400's speed, but it did not need to. ATR focused on emphasizing low operating costs, especially on short sectors where higher speed conferred little real-world advantage. The ATR was lighter, burned less fuel, and had lower maintenance costs. Airlines operating short hops of 200 to 400 kilometers found that ATR's balance of efficiency and reliability made more economic sense than the higher-speed Q400, which consumed more fuel and required more complex maintenance. Thus, the market gradually bifurcated: ATR became the champion of short-haul, high-frequency routes, while the Q400 carved out a niche on longer regional sectors where speed could be monetized.

The rivalry, however, was never purely about the aircraft. It was also about the corporate strategies behind them. Bombardier, as the owner of de Havilland and later the full Dash 8 program, was a diversified aerospace giant. It built everything from business jets to regional jets, and at one point even aimed to produce larger airliners through the CSeries program. ATR, on the other hand, was laser-focused: it made only one type of aircraft, in two sizes. This difference in focus shaped how each company engaged with the market. Bombardier could cross-sell turboprops with regional jets like the CRJ, appealing to airlines looking for a full product family. ATR, lacking this breadth, doubled down on building intimate partnerships and positioning itself as the specialist in turboprops.

During the 1990s and 2000s, market consolidation reshaped the competitive landscape. Fokker, once a strong player with its F27 turboprop and F70 and F100 regional jets, collapsed in 1996. British Aerospace and its ATP program exited the turboprop business. Saab ceased production of its 340 and 2000 regional aircraft in the late 1990s. Fairchild Dornier, which tried to compete with regional jets like the 328JET, went bankrupt in the early 2000s. In each case, the economic pressures of globalization and the rising dominance of jets eroded the viability of many smaller manufacturers. ATR and

Bombardier were left as the last two significant players in the turboprop segment.

This duopoly had profound implications. Airlines seeking new turboprops essentially had two choices: ATR or Bombardier. Over time, ATR won the larger share, consistently capturing the majority of new orders. The reasons were multifaceted. ATR's aircraft were cheaper to acquire and operate, making them attractive to cost-sensitive regional carriers. They also benefited from the backing of Airbus, which, after corporate restructuring in the 2000s, became a key shareholder. Airbus's global sales and marketing reach gave ATR a level of access and credibility that other regional manufacturers could not match.

Bombardier's focus became increasingly divided. The company invested heavily in its CRJ regional jets, which were highly successful in North America, and in its ambitious CSeries program, which eventually overwhelmed its finances. The Dash 8 line, while technologically impressive, began to appear peripheral to Bombardier's long-term strategy. Production volumes declined, and support for the program appeared inconsistent compared to ATR's steady, focused growth. This imbalance widened as ATR accumulated backlogs of hundreds of aircraft, while Bombardier struggled to secure consistent sales for the Q400.

The global financial crisis of 2008 further accentuated the divide. Regional airlines, under pressure to cut costs, favored the more economical ATRs over the faster but more expensive Q400s. Bombardier's sales faltered, while ATR managed to weather the downturn by capitalizing on its reputation for efficiency. The crisis underscored ATR's strategic advantage: by keeping its aircraft simple, lightweight, and optimized for short-haul economics, it had built resilience against volatile fuel prices and shrinking airline margins.

As the 2010s progressed, Bombardier's corporate troubles deepened. The CSeries program consumed vast amounts of capital, leading to financial distress and forcing the company to sell or spin off divisions. In 2019, Bombardier sold the Dash 8 program to Longview Aviation Capital, the parent company of Viking Air, which rebranded the aircraft under the historic de Havilland Canada name. ATR, meanwhile, remained steady under the joint ownership of Airbus and Leonardo (the successor of Aeritalia and Alenia). This shift effectively ended the era of direct rivalry between Bombardier and ATR. The Q400, while still supported and produced in limited numbers, no longer had the same corporate backing or market momentum. ATR emerged as the undisputed leader in the turboprop sector.

The decline of its main competitor did not mean ATR could rest on its laurels. The market itself was changing. Regional jets, particularly the Embraer E-Jet family, had captured significant market share, especially in North America. Passenger perceptions also favored jets in many regions, associating them with speed and modernity. ATR had to counter these perceptions by emphasizing environmental efficiency and passenger comfort. The launch of the ATR 600 series, with upgraded cabins and avionics, was part of this strategy. By modernizing the product while retaining its cost advantage, ATR ensured that it remained competitive not only against other turboprops but also against regional jets.

Consolidation also brought opportunities. As other turboprop manufacturers exited, ATR's used-aircraft market flourished. Airlines that might once have turned to Saab or Fokker for second-hand aircraft increasingly relied on ATRs. Leasing companies, seeing the strong demand for ATRs in emerging markets, built significant fleets of both new and used aircraft. This secondary market further entrenched ATR's dominance by ensuring that its aircraft remained visible and accessible even in lower-income regions.

In addition, ATR capitalized on Bombardier's retreat by pursuing niches where the Q400 once held sway. Airlines that had relied on the higher-speed Dash 8 found themselves with fewer options as de Havilland scaled back production. ATR seized the chance to highlight the versatility of its aircraft, including new freighter conversions and cargo-specific models that expanded its utility. By diversifying its applications, ATR not only absorbed market share from Bombardier but also positioned itself for growth in emerging sectors like regional cargo.

The consolidation of the regional aircraft market also underscored ATR's unusual position in global aviation. Unlike Embraer or Bombardier, ATR never tried to move up into jets. Unlike smaller manufacturers, it never spread itself too thin across multiple programs. This singular focus—turboprops for short-haul routes—was both a limitation and a strength. It meant ATR had no fallback if the turboprop market collapsed, but it also meant that every strategic decision, every investment, and every innovation was concentrated on a single goal. This clarity of purpose, combined with supportive ownership, enabled ATR to outlast many competitors.

Looking back, the rivalry between ATR and Bombardier shaped not just their own trajectories but the entire turboprop segment. The Dash 8 pushed ATR to innovate, ensuring that it did not stagnate. ATR's efficiency, in turn, pressured Bombardier to refine the Q400 into a highly capable but ultimately more expensive niche product. This dynamic competition raised the bar for regional aviation, benefiting airlines and passengers alike. In the end, however, the economics of aviation favored ATR's approach. By aligning itself with the cost-sensitive needs of regional carriers, it captured the broadest slice of the market and emerged as the survivor in a consolidated industry.

Today, ATR's dominance is both a triumph and a challenge. With few direct rivals remaining, it faces less competitive pressure but also bears the burden of sustaining innovation to keep turboprops relevant in an era increasingly defined by environmental goals and new propulsion technologies. The story of competition and consolidation, however, remains central to understanding ATR's identity: a company forged in rivalry, tested in crises, and ultimately sustained by its focus while others lost theirs.

Chapter 20: The Next Generation – ATR 600 Series

By the early years of the 21st century, ATR had secured its place as the world's leading turboprop manufacturer. Its aircraft, the ATR 42 and ATR 72, had proven reliable, efficient, and adaptable across a range of environments, from Europe's dense regional networks to Asia's island-hopping corridors. Yet success also bred risk. Aviation was changing, and passengers' expectations were evolving just as rapidly as airline economics. Airlines were under pressure to deliver not only efficiency but also a passenger experience that could compete with jets. Regulators were demanding ever-greater safety standards. Competitors, though diminished in number, were pushing boundaries of speed and technology. Against this backdrop, ATR faced a question that would define its next decades: how to keep its venerable product line relevant in a market hungry for innovation.

The answer came in the form of the ATR 600 series, a comprehensive modernization of both the ATR 42 and ATR 72. Launched in 2007, with the ATR 72-600 as its flagship, the program represented far more than a simple update. It was a deliberate effort to reposition ATR's turboprops for the 21st century, addressing both airline economics and passenger perceptions. The company knew it could not rely indefinitely on the original designs of the 1980s, however well they had aged. The 600 series had to show that turboprops could be every bit as modern as jets, while retaining the economic advantages that had made them indispensable.

At the heart of the ATR 600 series was the cockpit. Aviation technology had leaped forward in the decades since the

ATR's original debut, and pilots increasingly expected digital avionics as standard. ATR responded with a new glass cockpit designed by Thales, incorporating modern LCD screens, intuitive displays, and advanced flight management systems. Gone were the analogue dials and gauges of the earlier models, replaced by a suite of electronics that reduced workload, improved situational awareness, and brought ATR's turboprops into alignment with the technology found in larger Airbus and Boeing aircraft. The transition to a digital flight deck was not merely cosmetic; it provided tangible operational benefits, from better navigation precision to easier integration with modern air traffic management systems. For airlines, this meant smoother pilot training, particularly when transitioning crews between different aircraft types.

The engines, too, received significant attention. ATR partnered with Pratt & Whitney Canada to equip the 600 series with upgraded PW127M engines, offering increased power, improved efficiency, and enhanced reliability. This gave the aircraft better performance on hot-and-high routes, addressing one of the criticisms that had occasionally tilted the balance toward Bombardier's Q400 in certain markets. With more powerful engines, ATR's aircraft could operate from shorter runways and handle challenging conditions without sacrificing their hallmark efficiency. Airlines flying into difficult airports in India, Indonesia, or Latin America found the improvements especially valuable.

But perhaps the most visible transformation was inside the cabin. Passengers had long compared turboprops unfavorably with jets, perceiving them as noisier, less comfortable, and less modern. ATR recognized that winning hearts and minds required a reimagining of the cabin experience. The result was the Armonia cabin, introduced with the ATR 600 series. Designed by Italian firm Giugiaro, known for its automotive design expertise, Armonia aimed to change the narrative around turboprops. The cabin featured new slimline seats, larger overhead bins, LED lighting, and improved sound insulation. The combination of brighter interiors, quieter environments, and more ergonomic seating made the passenger experience far more appealing. Airlines could tailor the cabin layout to their markets, from high-density commuter setups to more spacious regional configurations.

The noise reduction effort was especially critical. Historically, propeller-driven aircraft had suffered from passenger complaints about cabin noise and vibration. ATR addressed this with advanced propeller technology, improved insulation, and refined cabin acoustics. By lowering the perceived noise level, the 600 series not only improved passenger comfort but also reduced the stigma that often accompanied turboprop travel. Marketing campaigns emphasized that modern turboprops were not the noisy machines of the past but sophisticated, comfortable aircraft well-suited to regional journeys.

Certification of the ATR 72-600 came in 2011, followed shortly by the ATR 42-600. Launch customers included Air New Zealand, Azul of Brazil, and Royal Air Maroc, each of which highlighted the aircraft's advantages in their respective markets. Air New Zealand, already a long-standing ATR operator, praised the 600 series for its ability to serve short domestic routes with efficiency and reliability, while offering passengers a noticeably improved onboard experience. Azul, an ambitious Brazilian carrier founded by JetBlue's David Neeleman, leveraged the ATR 72-600 to build its extensive domestic network, linking secondary cities and stimulating new demand. Royal Air Maroc used the aircraft to enhance connectivity within Morocco and across regional African markets.

The commercial reception of the 600 series confirmed that ATR had chosen the right path. Airlines valued not only the reduced fuel burn—an advantage that grew increasingly important as oil prices fluctuated in the 2010s—but also the modernized flight deck and cabin. Leasing companies, too, saw strong demand for the aircraft, recognizing its broad appeal across both mature and emerging markets. ATR's backlog swelled, and production rates climbed to meet demand.

The 600 series also enabled ATR to strengthen its hand in regions where the Q400 had previously held sway. The more powerful engines allowed ATR to compete more effectively on performance, while the cabin upgrades reduced the passenger comfort gap. Airlines weighing the higher-speed Q400 against the more economical ATR 72-600 increasingly found the ATR's combination of lower acquisition cost, lower operating cost, and now comparable comfort hard to resist. By the mid-2010s, ATR had cemented its dominance in the global turboprop market, with a market share often exceeding 75 percent of new orders.

The modernization also had important implications for training and operations. With a cockpit more closely aligned to Airbus standards, ATR could benefit from Airbus's global training ecosystem. Pilots found the transition between ATRs and other Airbus aircraft smoother, enhancing operational flexibility for airlines that operated mixed fleets. The 600 series also introduced modern maintenance and diagnostic systems, reducing downtime and helping airlines improve dispatch reliability.

Another significant aspect of the 600 series was its alignment with broader industry trends toward environmental efficiency. Airlines and regulators were increasingly focused on reducing carbon emissions, and ATR positioned the 600 series as the green choice for regional aviation. By highlighting its lower fuel burn compared to jets and even to rival turboprops, ATR tapped into a narrative that resonated with both airlines and governments. In some cases, airlines explicitly marketed their use of ATR 600 series aircraft as a sustainability measure, appealing to environmentally conscious travelers.

As the decade progressed, ATR continued to refine the 600 series. Optional features such as in-flight entertainment and connectivity were added, addressing passenger demand for digital experiences even on short flights. Cabin customization expanded, allowing airlines to differentiate their product. Cargo-focused variants, such as the ATR 72-600F freighter, were developed to meet growing demand in the e-commerce and logistics sectors. This adaptability extended the 600 series beyond passenger transport, ensuring that it remained relevant across a wide spectrum of aviation needs.

The success of the 600 series also had symbolic importance. It demonstrated that ATR, often seen as a niche player, could deliver a truly modern aircraft capable of competing on equal terms with larger manufacturers. The program reinvigorated ATR's brand, ensuring that it was not perceived as a relic of the past but as an innovator shaping the future of regional aviation. By investing in incremental improvements rather than radical redesigns, ATR maintained affordability and continuity, qualities highly valued by regional airlines operating on thin margins.

Yet the launch of the 600 series also raised questions about the future. Could incremental modernization sustain ATR indefinitely, or would the company eventually need to design a clean-sheet aircraft? The rise of hybrid and electric propulsion technologies hinted at a coming transformation in regional aviation. While the 600 series secured ATR's leadership in the present, it also set the stage for debates about what would follow. For the time being, however, airlines around the world embraced the 600 series as the gold standard in turboprop efficiency and reliability.

By the end of the 2010s, the ATR 600 series was flying with more than 200 airlines in over 100 countries. It connected remote communities in the Pacific, linked secondary cities in Europe, and shuttled commuters across India's expanding regional network. In Africa, it provided lifelines to towns far from major hubs. In Latin America, it climbed over mountains and across rainforests to connect people and economies. Each flight reinforced the aircraft's reputation as a workhorse of global aviation, a machine both humble and essential.

The ATR 600 series thus stands as a pivotal chapter in the company's history. It was not a radical departure but a thoughtful evolution, one that balanced tradition with innovation. By modernizing its aircraft without losing sight of its core values—efficiency, reliability, and adaptability—ATR ensured its continued relevance in a turbulent industry. The 600 series became not just a product but a statement: that turboprops still had a future, and that ATR would be the one to define it.

Chapter 21: Short Runways and Remote Routes

The global aviation network is often visualized as a web of gleaming international hubs—airports with long runways, sophisticated terminals, and the infrastructure to handle everything from widebody jets to the largest freighters. Yet the true backbone of air travel lies far beyond these marquee gateways. Thousands of smaller airfields, many with runways shorter than 1,200 meters, rough surfaces, or minimal ground facilities, form the lifelines of communities scattered across mountains, forests, deserts, and islands. For these airports, the aircraft that serve them must combine rugged design, nimble performance, and economic efficiency. This is the environment in which ATR has thrived, building its reputation as the world's most reliable short-field operator and proving indispensable in regions where other aircraft simply cannot land.

From the earliest days of the ATR 42's operations, short runway capability was not an afterthought but a central pillar of the aircraft's design philosophy. Regional aviation demanded it. Many of the communities that ATR sought to serve in Europe during the 1980s—small towns in France, Italy, Spain, and Scandinavia—relied on airstrips that were nowhere near the length of the runways in Paris or Rome. When ATR engineers set about designing their new turboprop, they emphasized a low takeoff and landing speed, robust landing gear, and strong brakes, all of which would allow the aircraft to operate safely on runways considered marginal for jets.

The ATR 42 in particular emerged as a specialist for short runways. With its lighter frame, powerful engines, and relatively low approach speed, it could land on strips as short as 800 meters, making it an invaluable tool for airlines serving remote communities. This opened the door to markets that jets could not dream of serving. While the ATR 72 required longer runways, it too outperformed most competitors in terms of field performance. Over time, both models gained certifications for operations from gravel and semi-prepared surfaces, further cementing their reputation as rugged workhorses.

One of the most striking illustrations of this came in the Caribbean. Islands such as Saint Barthélemy, Dominica, and Saba are notorious among pilots for their challenging airports. Gustaf III Airport in Saint Barthélemy features a runway of just 650 meters, with a steep hill at one end and the sea at the other. While only small commuter aircraft can land there regularly, ATRs became fixtures across other islands where runways measured just over a kilometer, and where the ability to take off fully loaded in hot conditions was crucial. The same held true in the Pacific, where Vanuatu, Fiji, and Papua New Guinea demanded aircraft that could reach island communities without long or paved runways. In these contexts, ATR became not just an airline asset but a community lifeline.

Another defining geography for ATR's short-field performance was the Indonesian archipelago. With more than 17,000 islands, many of which depend on air links for medical, educational, and economic access, Indonesia required aircraft that could land almost anywhere. ATR's turboprops became the backbone of airlines such as Lion Air's subsidiary Wings Air, serving destinations with runways barely more than a strip of asphalt carved into a coastal town or valley. The aircraft's ability to operate safely under such conditions gave it an unrivaled role in knitting together the sprawling archipelago.

ATR's dominance in short-field and remote-route operations was not limited to tropical or island environments. In Scandinavia, the aircraft became indispensable for serving remote northern communities in Norway, Sweden, and Finland. Many of these airports were built to modest specifications, sometimes with icy or snow-packed surfaces during winter. ATR's strong braking performance, high-mounted wings that minimized the risk of ice ingestion, and rugged undercarriage proved ideally suited to the conditions. Widerøe, Norway's iconic regional airline, built much of its identity around ATRs, flying them into fjord-bound airports where only the nimblest turboprops could operate consistently.

In mountainous regions, too, ATR proved itself repeatedly. Nepal is perhaps the most famous example. Tribhuvan International Airport in Kathmandu is the country's primary hub, but much of Nepal's aviation activity takes place at tiny airfields perched precariously in the Himalayas. Lukla Airport, gateway to Mount Everest, is famous for its 527-meter runway with a gradient of 12 percent, but other Nepali airports also present unique challenges: high altitude, steep terrain, unpredictable weather, and limited infrastructure.

While smaller aircraft dominate the most extreme strips, ATRs found a role in connecting larger provincial towns, operating reliably from airfields surrounded by peaks. Similarly, in Latin America, ATRs flew into airports like La Paz in Bolivia, Cusco in Peru, and countless others in Colombia and Ecuador, where high altitudes and short runways required specialized performance.

Underlying ATR's success in such places was a design philosophy that prioritized ruggedness. The landing gear was engineered to withstand repeated operations on less-than-ideal surfaces. The propeller system allowed for quick power adjustments during approaches, enabling stable descents into airports with steep approaches. Low approach speeds reduced the kinetic energy upon landing, minimizing runway requirements and wear on brakes. Taken together, these features allowed ATRs to consistently meet performance margins where other aircraft struggled or were prohibited altogether.

Economics played a role as well. Many of the airports with short runways also had limited passenger demand—sometimes only a handful of flights per day with 30 to 70 passengers on board. A jet, even if it could physically land, would not be economical. The ATR's low operating cost, high dispatch reliability, and ability to generate profits on sectors of fewer than 300 nautical miles made it uniquely suited to these markets. For governments seeking to subsidize essential air services, ATR offered the best balance of affordability and capability.

In some countries, the aircraft became almost synonymous with regional connectivity. In the Philippines, Cebu Pacific's Cebgo subsidiary built a network of ATR 72 flights linking small island airports to Manila and Cebu. For countless passengers, an ATR was their first experience of air travel, providing affordable and reliable service where ferries once took hours or even days. In the Pacific islands, airlines such as Air Tahiti and Air Calédonie became inseparable from their ATR fleets, connecting communities spread over vast ocean distances. The sight of an ATR at the gate became a familiar reassurance that even the most remote islands were not cut off from the wider world.

ATR's ability to serve such markets also gave it strategic importance in national aviation policies. In India, for example, the government's UDAN (Ude Desh ka Aam Nagrik) scheme launched in 2016 sought to improve regional connectivity by subsidizing flights to under-served airports. Many of these airfields had short runways unsuitable for jets, but ATRs could operate comfortably within the constraints. Airlines such as Alliance Air and IndiGo deployed ATR 72-600s to fulfill the program's goals, making ATR a key player in India's push to democratize air travel.

Similarly, in Africa, many nations relied on ATRs to ensure national cohesion. Countries such as Madagascar, where road travel between major towns can take days, depended heavily on ATRs for domestic connectivity. Air Madagascar, and later Tsaradia, used the aircraft extensively to reach airports that would otherwise remain isolated. In West Africa, carriers like ASKY Airlines and Air Burkina built networks of

ATR operations that linked secondary cities where infrastructure remained limited. These aircraft often carried not only passengers but also essential cargo, from medical supplies to school materials, reinforcing their role as lifelines rather than mere commercial assets.

The ATR's record on short runways also contributed significantly to its reputation among pilots. Flying into marginal airports requires skill, judgment, and confidence in one's machine. Pilots praised the ATR for its responsive controls, predictable handling, and robust systems, qualities that made it a trusted companion in demanding environments. Training programs emphasized the aircraft's short-field techniques, including steep approaches and rapid deceleration, which became part of the professional pride of ATR crews worldwide.

As the ATR 600 series entered service, these capabilities were further enhanced. The upgraded avionics provided greater precision in navigation, particularly valuable for approaches into airports without advanced instrument landing systems. Enhanced braking systems and more powerful engines expanded performance margins even further. Airlines flying into short or remote fields found that the 600 series not only maintained ATR's reputation but elevated it, providing crews with modern tools to complement the aircraft's rugged DNA.

The importance of short-runway operations cannot be overstated in understanding ATR's global dominance. While much of aviation's glamour lies in transcontinental jets, the true measure of connectivity lies in whether small towns, remote islands, and mountain valleys can access the national and international economy. ATR carved its niche here, making itself indispensable to communities where no alternative existed. Every landing on a short strip reinforced the aircraft's role not just as a machine but as a bridge between isolation and opportunity.

By the 2020s, ATRs had landed in more than 1,500 airports worldwide, many of which could not accommodate jets. This statistic underscores the company's achievement: without ATR, vast swathes of the globe would remain disconnected. In places where the only alternatives were boats, buses, or no travel at all, the ATR brought mobility, commerce, and hope. Its reputation as the champion of short runways and remote routes was not a marketing slogan but a lived reality, proven day after day in the skies of Asia, Africa, Latin America, and beyond.

Chapter 22: Training, Pilots, and Operations

Every successful aircraft is more than a feat of engineering; it is also a product of the men and women who fly it, maintain it, and train future generations to do the same. For ATR, whose global presence stretches across more than one hundred countries, the human dimension has always been as important as the technical one. The company's aircraft thrive in some of the most diverse and challenging operating environments in the world, from the frozen fjords of northern Norway to the dense tropical airstrips of Papua New Guinea. To succeed, ATR has had to build not only airplanes but also a comprehensive training and operations ecosystem that ensured safety, efficiency, and reliability no matter where the turboprops flew.

When the ATR 42 entered service in 1985, many airlines were new to regional turboprop operations. Training pilots to fly the new type was an immediate priority. Early courses were held in Toulouse, where ATR had established its headquarters and final assembly line. The company's vision was clear: it could not simply deliver aircraft and leave operators to figure out the rest. It had to act as a partner, equipping airlines with the skills and infrastructure necessary to operate safely. This philosophy gave rise to ATR's global training network, which over the decades would expand into one of the most respected turboprop training ecosystems in aviation.

Central to ATR's approach was the full flight simulator. These sophisticated devices replicate every aspect of an aircraft's performance, allowing pilots to practice complex scenarios in a safe, controlled environment. ATR invested early in simulators for both the ATR 42 and ATR 72, and Toulouse became the focal point for initial training. Crews would travel from across the world to France, spending weeks immersed in classroom instruction and simulator sessions before returning to their home airlines ready to operate.

As ATR deliveries spread across Europe, Asia, Africa, and the Americas, the need for localized training became clear. Airlines could not always afford to send their entire pilot corps to France, nor was it practical to rely on a single location. Thus, ATR partnered with training organizations and airlines to establish regional centers. By the 1990s, simulators were installed in Paris, Bangkok, and Miami, among other cities, making pilot training more accessible and reducing costs for operators. Each new training hub reinforced ATR's strategy: support airlines wherever they flew, tailoring programs to local needs.

The content of training went beyond basic type ratings. Operating turboprops, particularly in the kinds of environments ATR specialized in, required a different mindset than flying jets. Pilots had to master short-field landings, steep approaches, and operations from airports with minimal navigational aids. Weather added another layer of complexity, from heavy crosswinds in coastal airports to the turbulence of mountain valleys. ATR's simulators allowed crews to rehearse these exact scenarios, building muscle memory and decision-making skills that could mean the difference between a safe flight and an incident.

One of the most distinctive features of ATR's training curriculum was the emphasis on handling characteristics unique to turboprops. Unlike jets, turboprops have propeller-driven engines that require precise management of power settings, propeller pitch, and torque. The ATR's cockpit, with its characteristic overhead engine controls, demanded specific knowledge. Pilots transitioning from jets often had to adjust their instincts, particularly during takeoff and approach phases. ATR instructors emphasized these differences, ensuring that pilots did not assume turboprops were simply "small jets" but understood their unique flight dynamics.

As the company grew, so did its commitment to training infrastructure. The establishment of ATR Training Centres became a hallmark of the brand. In 2011, ATR inaugurated its flagship training center in Toulouse-Blagnac, equipped with multiple full flight simulators, flight training devices, and classrooms. The facility could handle thousands of pilot training hours annually, reflecting ATR's recognition that human expertise was as critical as aircraft production. Additional training centers followed in Paris, Singapore, and Miami, each serving as hubs for their respective regions.

Singapore, in particular, became a cornerstone of ATR's Asia-Pacific operations. With airlines like Lion Air, Wings Air, and IndiGo operating hundreds of ATRs, demand for training was immense. The Singapore center hosted not only simulators but also maintenance training, cabin crew instruction, and advanced courses in flight operations management. For Asia's booming regional aviation market,

ATR's investment in training infrastructure ensured that growth could be sustained safely and efficiently.

Pilots trained on ATR aircraft often spoke of the transition as both challenging and rewarding. The aircraft's responsive handling required precision but rewarded good technique. Instructors emphasized energy management—knowing how to control speed and descent rate to land safely on short runways. This discipline made ATR pilots highly skilled aviators, comfortable operating in conditions that would test even the most experienced crews. Airlines valued this not just for safety, but also because it cultivated a sense of professionalism and pride among ATR operators.

The company also invested in recurrent training, ensuring that crews remained sharp long after their initial qualification. Regulations required pilots to undergo simulator checks every six months, and ATR's global training centers facilitated this. Beyond mandatory checks, ATR developed specialized modules on subjects like low-visibility operations, performance-based navigation, and upset recovery. These programs kept crews at the cutting edge of operational best practices, reinforcing ATR's reputation for reliability and safety.

Beyond pilots, ATR recognized that safe operations required a holistic approach encompassing mechanics, flight dispatchers, and cabin crews. Maintenance training programs taught engineers how to service the unique features of turboprop engines, landing gear, and avionics. Cabin crew courses emphasized rapid evacuation procedures, adapted to the smaller cabin layouts of ATR aircraft. Flight dispatchers received instruction in performance calculations for short runways and high-altitude airports. Together, these programs ensured that every link in the operational chain was prepared for the realities of regional aviation.

In many cases, ATR's training programs transformed local aviation cultures. In countries like Myanmar, Madagascar, and Papua New Guinea, ATR worked closely with national carriers to develop training pipelines for pilots who might otherwise never have had access to advanced aviation instruction. By building local expertise, ATR helped strengthen aviation safety standards across entire regions. This investment in people was as important to ATR's global success as the aircraft themselves.

The introduction of the ATR 600 series further advanced the training landscape. With modern avionics based on a glass cockpit layout, pilots needed to adapt to a different workflow. The new flight deck featured electronic displays, flight management systems, and enhanced situational awareness tools, more akin to those found on modern jets. ATR's training programs guided pilots through this transition, ensuring that they could take full advantage of the technological improvements without losing the core turboprop handling skills.

ATR's training philosophy also adapted to technological change in the training industry itself. Virtual reality and advanced flight training devices allowed for more cost-effective instruction. Computer-based training modules could be accessed remotely, reducing the need for pilots to travel long distances. ATR embraced these innovations, integrating them into its global network to make training more accessible and efficient.

The COVID-19 pandemic highlighted just how vital this adaptability was. As airlines grounded fleets and furloughed staff, training continuity became a challenge. ATR responded by accelerating the use of distance learning tools, allowing pilots to stay current with theoretical instruction even when simulators were inaccessible. When operations resumed, ATR's training centers played a critical role in requalifying thousands of pilots who needed to return to active duty.

At the operational level, ATR aircraft developed a reputation for being forgiving but demanding of discipline. Their resilience in challenging conditions made them a favorite among regional pilots, who often regarded ATR operations as a proving ground for their skills. In many airlines, young pilots began their careers on ATRs, learning the fundamentals of energy management, weather judgment, and short-field technique before progressing to jets. This career pathway underscored ATR's role not only in regional aviation but in the broader training of pilots worldwide.

Airlines that built their networks around ATRs often worked hand-in-hand with the manufacturer to develop bespoke operational procedures. For instance, in Indonesia, where many runways are surrounded by high terrain, ATR collaborated with local airlines to refine approach procedures tailored to specific airports. In Africa, where dispatch reliability was critical to lifeline services, ATR provided specialized support for maintenance crews to keep aircraft flying despite logistical challenges. These partnerships went beyond training sessions—they became operational collaborations that reinforced ATR's role as a trusted partner.

Even in regions where competition with jets was strongest, ATR's training and operational ecosystem gave it an edge. U.S. airlines that experimented with ATR operations, for example, appreciated the manufacturer's hands-on support in training pilots and adapting to regional dynamics. While ATR's commercial presence in America was limited compared to elsewhere, the company's commitment to comprehensive support earned respect among industry professionals.

Perhaps the most enduring testament to ATR's training and operational legacy is the safety record it helped build. While the aircraft faced challenges in its early decades, particularly with weather-related incidents, ATR consistently learned from experience and integrated those lessons into training. Pilots received clearer guidance on handling icing, wind shear, and other hazards. Maintenance crews were trained to spot early warning signs of technical issues. Over time, these efforts paid dividends, elevating ATR's safety reputation and making its aircraft some of the most trusted turboprops in service.

By the 2020s, ATR had trained tens of thousands of pilots, mechanics, and cabin crew members worldwide. Its network of training centers stood as a quiet but essential pillar of its global dominance. The aircraft's versatility, after all, could only be realized through human skill. The company's foresight in investing in training and operations infrastructure ensured that its airplanes were not just delivered but embedded successfully into the aviation ecosystems of more than a hundred nations.

The story of ATR training and operations, then, is not just about classrooms and simulators. It is about building confidence in aircraft that serve communities others cannot reach. It is about empowering pilots in remote corners of the world to fly with the same professionalism as their counterparts at major airlines. It is about fostering a culture of safety, resilience, and partnership that has carried ATR through decades of change. And above all, it is about recognizing that an aircraft is only as effective as the people who fly and maintain it.

ATR's mastery of training and operations reflects a broader truth about regional aviation: that success lies in more than design or economics. It lies in the seamless integration of machine and human, where aircraft performance meets pilot skill, maintenance expertise, and operational understanding. By nurturing this integration, ATR not only delivered airplanes but also built a global community of aviators dedicated to keeping the world's most remote regions connected.

Chapter 23: Economic Resilience and Market Survival

The aviation industry is among the most volatile of global businesses, constantly buffeted by the winds of economic cycles, fluctuating fuel prices, geopolitical tensions, and technological change. For ATR, a company whose fortunes were tied closely to the health of regional carriers, resilience was not merely desirable; it was essential. Unlike major aircraft manufacturers producing widebody jets for intercontinental carriers, ATR's niche was the regional turboprop market—a sector highly vulnerable to local economics, political instability, and sudden disruptions in travel demand. Yet across nearly four decades of continuous production, ATR not only survived but solidified its position as the global leader in turboprops. This survival owed much to the company's adaptability, conservative yet consistent strategy, and a product line that continually proved indispensable to communities and airlines alike.

From the late 1980s onward, ATR encountered multiple global recessions that tested its durability. The first was the economic slowdown of the early 1990s, when airlines around the world cut back on capacity and shelved fleet expansion. Regional airlines in Europe and North America, initially enthusiastic about ATR deliveries, faced rising costs and shrinking demand. Yet ATR aircraft still found a role because they were less expensive to operate than regional jets and more suited to short-haul, low-density routes. Airlines under pressure could scale down from jets to ATRs, retaining connectivity without hemorrhaging money on under-filled aircraft. This adaptability proved a recurring theme in ATR's resilience strategy: when the market contracted, ATR's value proposition became even more compelling.

Fuel prices emerged as another recurring factor shaping the company's survival. In the late 1990s and early 2000s, oil prices fluctuated wildly, squeezing airline profit margins. Regional jets, which had proliferated in the 1990s as many carriers sought faster and more glamorous alternatives to turboprops, suddenly revealed their Achilles' heel: high fuel consumption on short routes. An ATR 72 burned up to 40 percent less fuel than a comparable regional jet, and as oil prices spiked, that difference translated into substantial savings. Many airlines that had sidelined turboprops returned to ATR as a hedge against volatile fuel costs. This cyclical rediscovery of the turboprop's efficiency underlined ATR's ability to not just survive downturns, but to emerge stronger when conditions favored fuel thrift over speed.

One of the starkest tests came with the financial crisis of 2008. Air travel demand collapsed, credit markets froze, and aircraft orders across the industry were delayed or canceled. Yet ATR endured, partly because regional aviation was less exposed to international travel slumps. Domestic connectivity remained essential, and ATR's lower operating costs allowed airlines to continue flying routes that would otherwise have been abandoned. Indeed, while widebody manufacturers like Boeing and Airbus struggled with deferred orders, ATR managed to maintain deliveries at a steady pace. In some cases, airlines even accelerated their shift back to turboprops, recognizing that survival depended on trimming fuel bills and operating smaller, more flexible aircraft.

Crucial to ATR's resilience was its ability to balance conservative growth with adaptability. The company never attempted to compete directly in the regional jet market, leaving that battle to Bombardier, Embraer, and later Mitsubishi. Instead, ATR stayed laser-focused on turboprops, refining the ATR 42 and 72 families rather than chasing risky new ventures. This disciplined approach meant ATR avoided the costly missteps that often plagued aircraft programs. While Bombardier poured billions into the CSeries jet (later taken over by Airbus as the A220), ATR maintained profitability with incremental improvements and reliable support for its existing customer base. That stability reassured operators and investors, reinforcing confidence in ATR as a dependable partner through turbulent times.

Another dimension of resilience lay in ATR's global spread. By diversifying its customer base across Europe, Asia, Africa, and Latin America, ATR insulated itself from regional downturns. When economic trouble hit one part of the world, another region often experienced growth. For example, during the Asian financial crisis of the late 1990s, demand in Europe and Latin America helped sustain production. Similarly, when Latin American economies faltered in the 2010s, Asia-Pacific orders surged as airlines in Indonesia, the Philippines, and India embraced ATR aircraft to support booming domestic travel. This geographic diversity became a cornerstone of ATR's survival, preventing over-reliance on any single market.

The company also demonstrated resilience by navigating airline bankruptcies, an unavoidable feature of regional aviation. Carriers like Air Littoral in France, TAT in Europe, and countless small operators in Asia and Africa disappeared over the decades, sometimes leaving ATR with fleets stranded or contracts unfulfilled. Yet the aircraft themselves rarely went to waste. Thanks to their durability and strong resale value, ATRs could be quickly redeployed with new operators. Leasing companies and secondary markets thrived on ATR aircraft, giving them second, third, and even fourth lives. This circular economy ensured that production lines could continue even if initial customers failed; the aircraft's long lifespan meant that someone, somewhere, would find use for it.

Partnership with leasing companies became particularly important in ensuring resilience. Lessors such as Nordic Aviation Capital and Avation PLC developed vast ATR portfolios, enabling airlines with limited capital to access aircraft through leases rather than outright purchase. This arrangement smoothed out the cyclical nature of demand. Even in downturns, airlines could downsize fleets without grounding aircraft permanently, while lessors could place those ATRs with carriers in more resilient markets. ATR's close cooperation with the leasing community thus acted as a buffer, sustaining production even when direct airline orders lagged.

Resilience also stemmed from ATR's continuous efforts to reduce operating costs and enhance reliability. Regional airlines typically run tight margins, and unexpected maintenance or inefficiency can be catastrophic. ATR invested steadily in product support, spare parts availability, and training programs, recognizing that the operational continuity of its customers directly affected its own survival. The company's Global Maintenance Agreement (GMA) program, introduced in the 2000s, offered airlines predictable maintenance costs and guaranteed support. This kind of partnership kept operators afloat during difficult times and reinforced long-term loyalty to ATR.

The battle with Bombardier's Dash 8 family provided a clear test of resilience. For decades, the Canadian manufacturer offered ATR its fiercest competition, particularly with the Dash 8 Q400, which boasted higher speeds and performance. Some analysts predicted ATR would struggle against the faster, jet-like Dash 8. Yet when oil prices surged and demand shifted toward efficiency, ATR's lower fuel burn proved decisive. The Dash 8 program dwindled, eventually ceasing production in 2021, while ATR retained its role as the dominant turboprop manufacturer. Survival here was not about being the flashiest but about sticking to fundamentals: efficiency, reliability, and affordability.

Resilience also had a cultural dimension. ATR cultivated a company ethos that emphasized steady, pragmatic decision-making rather than headline-grabbing risks. Engineers and managers understood that their niche was critical connectivity, not technological showmanship. While ATR experimented with innovations such as the ATR 600 series' glass cockpit and cabin upgrades, it never jeopardized its stability with over-ambitious programs. This culture of measured progress built trust among airlines that knew ATR would not abandon them in pursuit of radical gambles.

The COVID-19 pandemic provided perhaps the sternest test yet of ATR's survival instincts. With global travel collapsing in 2020, many regional carriers grounded their fleets, and ATR deliveries slowed sharply. Yet once again, the turboprop's efficiency and versatility offered a lifeline. Airlines converted ATRs into temporary freighters to serve e-commerce and medical supply chains. When passenger traffic began its uneven recovery, ATR aircraft were among the first to return to service, reconnecting short-haul routes that jets could not economically sustain. By 2021, as aviation's recovery accelerated, ATR's backlog and production line proved intact, a testament to its ability to withstand even unprecedented shocks.

Another aspect of resilience emerged in ATR's environmental positioning. As climate change debates intensified, governments and passengers scrutinized aviation's carbon footprint. Here again, ATR's efficiency became a shield. The company could credibly claim that its turboprops emitted far less carbon per passenger than regional jets. This narrative not only boosted its survival in a climate-conscious era but also positioned ATR for growth as airlines sought greener options. In effect, global concern over sustainability aligned perfectly with ATR's long-standing strengths.

Looking across the decades, ATR's story of resilience is not one of explosive growth or dramatic breakthroughs, but of consistency, adaptability, and enduring relevance. It survived downturns by sticking to its niche, weathered fuel crises by capitalizing on efficiency, and endured competition by outlasting rivals. It spread across global markets to avoid dependency and built strong ties with lessors and operators to ensure continuity. It reinforced its product support to keep customers loyal and adapted to shocks like the pandemic by pivoting quickly to new roles.

In many ways, ATR's survival reflects the very qualities of its aircraft. Just as the ATR 42 and 72 were designed to operate reliably in tough conditions, the company itself operated with rugged pragmatism, able to navigate turbulence without losing direction. The same attributes that made the turboprop indispensable to small communities—efficiency, adaptability, resilience—were mirrored in ATR's corporate strategy.

By the 2020s, ATR had become not just a survivor but the last major turboprop manufacturer standing, an achievement made possible by its resilience through four decades of economic storms. The company's ability to endure while rivals faltered underscored a fundamental truth of aviation: survival belongs not to those who chase speed or glamour, but to those who deliver consistent value in the real, often harsh, world of air transport. ATR had built a business not on fragile demand or speculative technologies, but on steady, reliable service—and in the turbulent skies of global aviation, that made all the difference.

Chapter 24: ATR in the COVID-19 Era

Few moments in aviation history tested the resilience and adaptability of the industry as severely as the COVID-19 pandemic. What began in early 2020 as a health crisis rapidly became a global economic shock, grounding fleets, collapsing passenger demand, and exposing structural vulnerabilities in airlines of every size. For ATR, a company whose reputation rested on providing indispensable regional connectivity, the pandemic presented both existential challenges and unexpected opportunities. Across the span of those turbulent years, ATR and its operators demonstrated how turboprops could adapt to a world where air travel patterns shifted almost overnight, and where survival demanded creativity, pragmatism, and resilience.

The sudden onset of the pandemic in early 2020 brought the aviation industry to a near standstill. International borders closed, domestic travel restrictions were enforced, and passengers simply stopped flying. Global air traffic fell by more than 60 percent within weeks, and even the most resilient airlines faced grounding of much of their fleets. For ATR operators, the situation was dire: regional carriers often served markets dependent on business and leisure travel, both of which vanished almost instantly. Aircraft that had been operating multiple daily flights were suddenly parked, with only skeleton services maintained to preserve essential connectivity. ATR deliveries, which had been steady at over 70 units annually, collapsed as airlines froze orders and leasing companies postponed placements. The assembly line in Toulouse, normally a steady hum of activity, slowed to a trickle.

Yet even in this darkest of periods, ATR's advantages became apparent. Regional connectivity did not disappear entirely, even during the strictest lockdowns. Governments, healthcare agencies, and essential businesses still required mobility for medical staff, supplies, and critical goods. Turboprops like the ATR 42 and 72, with their low operating costs and short takeoff and landing capabilities, were often the only economical choice for maintaining these lifelines. National carriers and small regional airlines alike pressed ATR aircraft into service for special missions: transporting medical workers to remote areas, carrying COVID-19 test samples and vaccines, or flying food supplies to isolated communities.

One of the most striking adaptations was the rapid conversion of ATRs into makeshift freighters. With passenger cabins empty and cargo demand surging due to the boom in e-commerce and medical logistics, airlines began removing seats from ATR cabins to create additional cargo space. Some operators, under emergency regulatory approvals, loaded boxes directly onto the cabin floor. Others used ATRs for "combi" missions, carrying freight in the cabin and belly hold while still accommodating a small number of essential passengers. These improvised solutions showcased the aircraft's flexibility, but they also highlighted an enduring strength: ATR's relatively low acquisition and operating costs made it possible for airlines to repurpose the aircraft quickly without prohibitive investment.

The pivot to cargo was not just temporary improvisation; it accelerated an ongoing trend toward freighter conversions. Even before the pandemic, ATR had developed a factory-built ATR 72-600F freighter model, aimed at the growing market for regional cargo. COVID-19 suddenly created an urgent real-world test case. Airlines and logistics companies recognized that smaller freighters were critical in serving short-haul, point-to-point cargo networks, particularly for e-commerce deliveries that bypassed traditional hub-and-spoke models. As global supply chains came under strain, ATR freighters proved invaluable in maintaining steady flows of goods. In many respects, the pandemic validated ATR's strategic bet on freighter conversions, positioning the company for sustained demand in the years to follow.

Beyond cargo, ATR operators found resilience in the aircraft's suitability for short, essential routes that remained viable during the crisis. While intercontinental travel collapsed, domestic and regional connectivity retained pockets of demand, particularly in archipelagic countries such as Indonesia and the Philippines, or in vast nations like India. Governments often subsidized these flights to preserve essential lifelines, and ATR operators were at the forefront of these efforts. In such environments, flying a regional jet with 90 or more seats would have been uneconomical, but a 40- to 70-seat turboprop could match the reduced demand while keeping costs manageable.

Financial survival during the pandemic was an enormous challenge for all airlines, but regional carriers had both vulnerabilities and advantages. On one hand, their margins were razor-thin, and sudden demand collapse was devastating. On the other hand, the relative affordability of turboprop operations provided some breathing space. ATR itself supported its customers through flexible maintenance programs and tailored service agreements, easing the immediate financial burden. The company worked closely with leasing companies to accommodate deferrals and maintain customer relationships, understanding that long-term survival depended on collaborative solutions rather than rigid enforcement of contracts.

Training and operations also faced disruption. With crews grounded and travel restrictions in place, pilot training became difficult. ATR responded by leveraging its global training centers and simulators in Toulouse, Paris, Miami, Johannesburg, and Singapore, adopting digital tools to provide remote training support. Virtual classroom environments allowed pilots to maintain currency on procedures, even if simulator sessions were delayed. This adaptation not only helped airlines through the crisis but also accelerated ATR's adoption of blended training models that would remain valuable in the post-pandemic era.

For ATR itself, the pandemic forced a painful recalibration of production and workforce management. In 2020, only a fraction of the planned deliveries could be completed, and staff reductions became unavoidable. The company, like the entire Airbus ecosystem, faced the challenge of scaling down without permanently damaging its industrial capability. Suppliers across Europe, many of which specialized in components for ATR aircraft, also struggled, but ATR worked to preserve its network by carefully balancing reduced production with continued support. This effort underscored the importance of maintaining supply chain health, a lesson that would resonate long after the pandemic receded.

Perhaps most significant was how COVID-19 reshaped the conversation around the future of regional aviation. Analysts noted that while global long-haul travel might take years to recover, domestic and regional markets were likely to rebound faster. Travelers, hesitant to embark on international journeys, were more willing to fly short-haul for family, work, or leisure within their own countries. This trend played directly to ATR's strengths. By 2021 and 2022, as vaccination campaigns expanded and restrictions eased, ATR operators were among the first to restore significant portions of their schedules. Turboprops, once derided by some passengers as outdated, now represented resilience: they were the aircraft that kept flying when almost everything else stopped.

The pandemic also dovetailed with ATR's narrative on sustainability. Airlines and governments alike began reconsidering the future of aviation in light of climate imperatives. With passenger demand uncertain, efficiency became more important than ever. ATR's turboprops, already burning significantly less fuel than regional jets, emerged as a natural bridge toward a greener aviation future. The company seized the opportunity to highlight its progress in sustainable aviation fuel (SAF) compatibility and its research into hybrid-electric propulsion. By aligning its product with both post-pandemic recovery and long-term environmental goals, ATR positioned itself as not merely a survivor of COVID-19, but a company equipped to thrive in the reshaped aviation landscape.

Case studies from across the world highlighted this dynamic. In Indonesia, Lion Air subsidiary Wings Air continued to operate ATR 72s to remote islands throughout the crisis, providing critical links for medical evacuations and essential goods. In Europe, carriers such as Silver Airways in the United States and Air Corsica in France relied on ATRs to sustain truncated domestic networks. In Africa, Air Senegal and others used ATRs to connect secondary cities when larger aircraft would have been untenable. In Latin America, airlines in the Caribbean demonstrated the aircraft's indispensability in serving small islands where alternatives were non-existent. Each example underscored that ATR was not merely an aircraft in service, but an enabler of continuity in a fragmented and disrupted world.

By 2022, as aviation demand began recovering unevenly across the globe, ATR faced the task of rebuilding its order book. While some airlines remained financially crippled, others recognized that the recovery provided an opportunity to recalibrate fleets. Many opted to renew with efficient turboprops, betting that short-haul travel would lead the rebound. Leasing companies again played a critical role, placing aircraft with airlines hesitant to commit capital but eager to restart operations. ATR's backlog stabilized, and production gradually returned toward pre-pandemic levels. The recovery was not uniform—regions such as Asia-Pacific bounced back faster than Europe—but ATR's global reach once again provided resilience.

The pandemic also deepened ATR's relationship with governments and policymakers. In many countries, regional aviation was recognized as a public good, vital for economic stability and social cohesion. Subsidies, relief programs, and strategic investments often flowed toward airlines operating ATR aircraft, underscoring the company's role in national resilience. ATR itself engaged in dialogues about how turboprops could serve as part of future-proofed, environmentally conscious aviation ecosystems. The alignment of economic survival with sustainability agendas created a powerful narrative that ATR skillfully leveraged.

Looking back, the COVID-19 era represented both disruption and transformation for ATR. The company endured one of the most severe downturns in aviation history, with production slashed and demand decimated. Yet ATR and its operators also demonstrated extraordinary adaptability: converting passenger aircraft to freighters, sustaining essential services, embracing digital training tools, and positioning turboprops as indispensable in both crisis response and recovery. By the time the industry stabilized in the mid-2020s, ATR had not only survived but reinforced its identity as the backbone of regional connectivity.

Ultimately, the pandemic reinforced the qualities that had defined ATR since its founding: resilience, pragmatism, and a focus on real-world utility. Just as ATR aircraft had weathered economic recessions, oil crises, and competitive threats in earlier decades, they now proved their worth in a once-in-a-century disruption. The lessons of COVID-19 shaped ATR's future strategy, reminding the company and its customers alike that survival depends not on speed or glamour, but on adaptability, efficiency, and an unshakable commitment to connecting communities—even in the most uncertain times.

Chapter 25: Hybrid Futures and Sustainable Aviation Fuel

As the aviation industry looked beyond the upheaval of the COVID-19 pandemic, it faced a challenge that was both older and more enduring: environmental sustainability. Long before 2020, concerns about carbon emissions, noise, and the ecological footprint of aviation had begun reshaping the global conversation. Governments, regulators, airlines, and manufacturers were all under increasing pressure to demonstrate progress toward greener skies. For ATR, a company whose turboprops were already recognized for their relative efficiency compared to regional jets, this pressure was both a challenge and an opportunity. The years following the pandemic accelerated ATR's efforts in hybrid-electric propulsion and sustainable aviation fuel (SAF), positioning the turboprop as a bridge between traditional aviation and a more sustainable future.

The starting point of ATR's environmental narrative was its existing efficiency advantage. Compared to regional jets of similar capacity, ATR aircraft consumed up to 40 percent less fuel on short-haul routes. This was not a new discovery—airlines had long appreciated the economic benefits of turboprop fuel efficiency—but as the environmental debate grew sharper, these same numbers acquired new meaning. In a world aiming for net-zero emissions by 2050, every percentage point of fuel savings translated into reduced carbon output and a stronger case for turboprops as an environmentally responsible choice. ATR leaned heavily on this advantage, framing its aircraft not only as economical but as inherently sustainable tools for regional mobility.

Yet efficiency alone was not enough. The aviation industry as a whole was committing to far more ambitious goals, including International Air Transport Association (IATA) pledges for net-zero emissions by mid-century. Governments in Europe, where environmental regulation was particularly stringent, pushed manufacturers to accelerate the adoption of new technologies. ATR, as part of the Airbus industrial ecosystem, was drawn directly into these efforts. Hybrid-electric propulsion and SAF compatibility became the cornerstones of ATR's strategy, not as futuristic ambitions but as near-term pathways to secure relevance in a rapidly evolving regulatory and commercial environment.

Sustainable aviation fuel represented the most immediate step. Unlike futuristic propulsion systems, SAF could be deployed in existing aircraft with minimal modification, provided engines and fuel systems were certified. ATR moved quickly to establish full compatibility across its fleet. By the early 2020s, ATR had achieved certification for operations with SAF blends of up to 50 percent, aligning with international standards. Demonstration flights were conducted using higher SAF ratios, including notable partnerships with airlines and fuel producers. These flights were more than symbolic—they demonstrated to regulators, governments, and passengers that ATR aircraft were ready to operate with dramatically reduced lifecycle emissions.

The promise of SAF lay in its potential to cut carbon emissions by as much as 80 percent compared to conventional kerosene, depending on the feedstock and production method. Bio-based SAF derived from waste oils, agricultural residues, or non-food crops offered one pathway; synthetic SAF produced through renewable energy and captured carbon represented another. ATR positioned itself as an enabler rather than a producer, working closely with suppliers and airlines to ensure that its aircraft would not be the bottleneck in adoption. In this sense, ATR's strategy was pragmatic: while acknowledging that SAF supply chains and costs remained obstacles, the company could at least guarantee that its aircraft were ready the moment the fuel became available at scale.

Parallel to SAF readiness, ATR invested in hybrid-electric propulsion research. Here the challenges were greater, but so too were the potential rewards. Electric propulsion promised not only reduced carbon emissions but also lower noise and operating costs—attributes highly attractive to regional operators flying into noise-sensitive airports or short-haul markets where fuel costs were a significant burden. ATR, together with partners including Airbus and engine manufacturers, began exploring configurations where electric or hybrid-electric systems could supplement traditional turboprops.

The concept of hybrid-electric ATRs was not science fiction; it was grounded in specific technical studies. One model envisioned a conventional turboprop engine supported by electric motors during takeoff and climb—the most energy-intensive phases of flight. This "boost" could reduce fuel burn significantly while also lowering noise. Another model explored the potential for fully electric taxiing, eliminating fuel consumption during ground operations. The modularity of the ATR platform, with its relatively simple systems compared to jets, made it an attractive candidate for experimentation.

By the mid-2020s, ATR had launched a program known as "ECO" (Electric Collaborative Operations), aimed at bringing hybrid-electric concepts from laboratory to testbed. Working with engine makers such as Pratt & Whitney Canada, ATR explored how its future turboprops might integrate electric assistance seamlessly, without sacrificing reliability or safety. These programs reflected a recognition that while full-electric 70-seat aircraft were unlikely in the near term due to battery limitations, hybrid systems could deliver meaningful emissions reductions much sooner.

The broader industry context was equally important. Regional aviation was increasingly recognized as a proving ground for green technologies. Unlike long-haul aircraft, which faced daunting challenges in adopting alternative fuels or propulsion due to their size and range, regional aircraft operated shorter sectors, where battery weight penalties and SAF logistics were more manageable. Policymakers saw regional aviation as the natural laboratory for innovation, and ATR embraced this role. By positioning its turboprops as platforms for experimentation and incremental adoption, ATR ensured its relevance in environmental debates that might otherwise have marginalized conventional manufacturers.

Airlines, too, played a role in driving demand for greener solutions. Carriers in Scandinavia, such as Widerøe of Norway, were particularly vocal in calling for sustainable regional aircraft, motivated both by national environmental goals and passenger expectations in environmentally conscious markets. Widerøe, an ATR operator, became a partner in several pilot projects exploring electric and hybrid propulsion. Elsewhere, airlines in France, Italy, and Canada joined demonstration programs, recognizing that public perception and regulatory pressure would increasingly favor those seen as pioneers in sustainability.

ATR's narrative also emphasized the social dimension of sustainability. By highlighting that its aircraft connected remote communities more efficiently and with less environmental impact than jets, ATR reframed turboprops not as outdated relics but as progressive tools. Marketing materials increasingly featured comparisons showing how an ATR flight consumed less fuel per passenger than equivalent road or ferry journeys in many regions. This framing was particularly effective in archipelagic countries, where air travel was essential but environmentally scrutinized. In this way, ATR demonstrated that sustainability was not just about global targets but about practical, localized benefits.

Still, challenges remained. SAF supply was limited, and costs were significantly higher than traditional kerosene. Hybrid-electric technologies were years away from certification and mass adoption. Critics argued that incremental improvements would not be enough to meet aviation's ambitious climate goals. ATR acknowledged these realities but argued that pragmatism was essential. While revolutionary technologies would take decades, immediate gains could be made by deploying SAF-ready, highly efficient turboprops across regional networks. The company framed its approach as evolutionary rather than revolutionary—realistic progress rather than speculative promises.

The strategy resonated with governments and airlines looking for practical solutions. In France, policy debates about banning short domestic flights where rail alternatives existed highlighted the scrutiny facing aviation. ATR's efficiency allowed airlines to defend routes that might otherwise have been politically vulnerable, arguing that the environmental cost was relatively low and could be further reduced with SAF. In developing countries, where rail infrastructure was limited, ATR positioned itself as the sustainable enabler of mobility, ensuring that environmental progress did not mean economic exclusion.

By the late 2020s, ATR's efforts were yielding tangible results. Airlines began operating regular flights with high SAF blends, often marketed to passengers as "green flights." Demonstration projects for hybrid-electric taxiing entered advanced testing. ATR's communications strategy highlighted these achievements, reinforcing the company's identity as the global leader in sustainable regional aviation. At industry conferences, ATR executives positioned the turboprop not as a transitional technology but as a central player in the aviation ecosystem of the future.

The ripple effects extended to leasing companies and financiers. As sustainability became a criterion for investment, aircraft with strong environmental credentials gained favor. ATR's fuel efficiency and SAF readiness made it attractive in this context, ensuring continued demand even as financiers became more selective. Leasing companies, always attuned to long-term asset value, recognized that an ATR equipped for SAF and hybrid upgrades would remain viable well into the 2040s.

Perhaps the most profound impact of ATR's environmental initiatives was cultural. For decades, turboprops had carried an image problem in some markets, perceived as noisy, slow, or outdated compared to sleek jets. By reframing the turboprop as the green choice—the aircraft that consumed less, emitted less, and pioneered hybrid solutions—ATR turned this perception on its head. Suddenly, choosing a turboprop was not a compromise but a statement of responsibility. Airlines embraced this message, integrating environmental branding into their marketing. Passengers, increasingly aware of their carbon footprints, began to see turboprop flights as the ethical option.

In reflecting on ATR's journey into hybrid futures and SAF, it becomes clear that the company's strategy combined pragmatism with vision. ATR did not claim to reinvent aviation overnight, nor did it ignore the magnitude of the sustainability challenge. Instead, it leaned into its strengths—efficiency, adaptability, and close ties with regional operators—while positioning itself as a testbed for emerging solutions. This balance allowed ATR to remain credible in both technical and policy debates, while maintaining commercial momentum.

By the early 2030s, as hybrid-electric prototypes advanced and SAF production scaled, ATR's foresight was evident. The company had weathered the turbulence of COVID-19 not by retreating but by aligning itself with the dominant theme of the era: sustainability. Its turboprops were no longer merely aircraft for regional routes; they had become symbols of a future where aviation could be both accessible and environmentally responsible. The narrative of hybrid futures and sustainable aviation fuel thus marked not just a chapter in ATR's history but a defining transformation—one that ensured its relevance for decades to come.

Chapter 26: A Global Icon of Regional Aviation

When historians of aviation look back on the closing decades of the twentieth century and the opening decades of the twenty-first, one name will inevitably recur when discussing regional connectivity: ATR. Few aircraft programs have so thoroughly shaped the experience of regional travel, not just in one country or continent but across the globe. From its origins in a Franco-Italian collaboration to its position as the world's leading regional turboprop manufacturer, ATR evolved into more than a maker of airplanes. It became a symbol of resilience, adaptability, and quiet dominance in an industry often defined by glamour at the long-haul end of the spectrum. Yet it was precisely in the quiet, short-haul markets—where most journeys actually took place—that ATR built its legacy.

ATR's story was one of persistence in a market where many competitors faltered. The turboprop sector had once been crowded: Fokker, Saab, British Aerospace, Dornier, Bombardier, and others had each vied for regional airline business. But one by one, they exited the market, victims of rising costs, shifting strategies, or simply the relentless economics of aircraft manufacturing. By the 2010s, ATR stood virtually alone, the only manufacturer offering new-build turboprops in large numbers. That survival was not an accident. It reflected a careful balancing act between innovation and conservatism, between the needs of developing nations and the expectations of advanced markets, and between the pressures of global competition and the realities of regional airline economics.

Central to ATR's identity was the fact that it built aircraft specifically designed for the missions they served. The ATR 42 and ATR 72 were not repurposed from larger airframes or cut-down versions of jets; they were optimized for short sectors, modest passenger loads, and challenging operating environments. That optimization gave them a ruggedness and flexibility that jets could not match. Whether operating from gravel strips in Papua, high-altitude airports in the Andes, or short runways on Mediterranean islands, ATRs proved capable and dependable. Airlines appreciated not only the performance but also the economics: operating costs were low, fuel efficiency was high, and the simplicity of the design kept maintenance manageable even in remote regions.

Over time, these advantages translated into a global footprint. ATRs became ubiquitous in Asia, particularly in countries like Indonesia and the Philippines where islands outnumber highways. In India, they became the backbone of government-sponsored regional connectivity programs. In Africa, ATRs connected communities separated by vast distances and poor infrastructure. In Latin America, they climbed mountain passes and threaded through jungle airstrips. Even in Europe, where high-speed rail and dense road networks offered alternatives, ATRs remained vital in linking islands, secondary cities, and underserved regions.

Such widespread adoption reshaped the perception of turboprops. Where once passengers might have viewed them as noisy, uncomfortable, or outdated, the modern ATR cabins of the 600 series presented a different picture. LED lighting, quieter interiors, larger luggage bins, and improved seating made ATR flights comparable in comfort to regional jets, while the efficiency advantage remained decisive. Airlines discovered that passenger resistance to turboprops diminished when the product was marketed not as a compromise but as the modern, sustainable choice. By the 2020s, this shift in perception was critical: environmental awareness meant that efficiency was a selling point in itself, and turboprops were increasingly celebrated as responsible rather than second-class travel.

ATR's status as a global icon also owed much to its partnerships with airlines. Unlike larger manufacturers that often focused on deals with flagship carriers, ATR's relationships were often with smaller, regional airlines that built their entire business models around turboprops. For many such carriers, the ATR was not simply a type in the fleet—it was the fleet. This intimacy created a degree of mutual dependence: ATR needed these airlines to sustain production, and the airlines needed ATR to provide continual support, upgrades, and training. The result was a global community where ATR had an unusually close connection to the operators of its aircraft. Training centers, maintenance support, and pilot programs reflected this emphasis, ensuring that operators in both developed and developing countries had access to the same quality of service.

The symbolic weight of ATR's aircraft was often greatest in places where alternatives were few. In small island nations in the Pacific or Caribbean, ATRs often represented the only reliable link to the outside world. They carried medical supplies, schoolchildren, government officials, and tourists alike, stitching together societies that might otherwise have been isolated. In landlocked regions of Africa, they performed similar functions, serving as literal lifelines. In such contexts, the ATR was not merely an aircraft—it was a social and economic enabler, a machine that underpinned connectivity, development, and opportunity.

Culturally, ATRs became part of the fabric of daily life in many of these regions. Passengers who had never flown on a Boeing 747 or an Airbus A380 had almost certainly boarded an ATR. For them, aviation was not about luxury or long-haul glamour but about reliable, affordable transport to the next city, the nearest hospital, or the regional capital. In this sense, ATR democratized flight. Its impact was measured not in prestige but in accessibility, making air travel routine for millions of people across the globe.

The company's survival through the turbulent decades of aviation also contributed to its iconic status. ATR weathered oil shocks, airline bankruptcies, shifting alliances, and global crises such as the COVID-19 pandemic. Where other manufacturers abandoned turboprops, ATR doubled down, refining its designs and reinforcing its value proposition. Its incremental approach—avionics upgrades here, cabin improvements there, efficiency tweaks with each generation—ensured the aircraft never felt obsolete. This philosophy of continuous evolution, rather than revolutionary but risky redesigns, preserved the ATR's competitiveness for nearly four decades.

Airbus's growing role in ATR's governance further anchored its position. By aligning itself with one of the largest aerospace groups in the world, ATR gained stability, marketing reach, and credibility. At the same time, its joint-venture structure with Italian partners ensured that ATR retained its identity as a specialized, nimble player within a vast ecosystem. This duality—a niche producer backed by a giant—gave ATR resilience that few competitors could match.

The environmental dimension of ATR's story crystallized its global image in the 2020s. As the aviation industry came under intense scrutiny for its contribution to climate change, ATR's message was clear: the turboprop was not a relic of the past but a technology for the future. SAF compatibility, hybrid-electric experiments, and unmatched fuel efficiency positioned ATR as the responsible choice. Airlines capitalized on this narrative, branding ATR flights as green journeys and framing their turboprop operations as acts of environmental stewardship. In doing so, they reinforced ATR's role not just as a practical solution but as a symbol of aviation's path toward sustainability.

Even competition played a role in shaping ATR's legacy. For decades, the Dash 8 from Bombardier had been the primary rival. When Bombardier exited the regional aircraft market, and the Dash 8 line passed into uncertain hands, ATR emerged as the uncontested leader. Far from weakening ATR's drive, the rivalry had sharpened its focus and pushed it toward continual improvement. Once alone at the top, ATR bore the responsibility of keeping turboprops relevant, and by most measures, it succeeded.

By the early 2030s, ATR's installed base exceeded 1,600 aircraft worldwide, flying with over 200 operators in more than 100 countries. These numbers reflected not just commercial success but geographical breadth unmatched by any regional aircraft program. No other manufacturer could claim such a universally distributed footprint. The sight of an ATR on a runway—whether in a European capital, a Pacific island, or an African hinterland—came to symbolize the very idea of regional aviation.

The legacy of ATR also extended beyond the aircraft themselves. Through training programs, maintenance partnerships, and industrial cooperation, ATR helped build aviation capacity in regions where it had been limited. In countries from Myanmar to Mauritania, ATR aircraft were the vehicles through which new generations of pilots, mechanics, and airline managers cut their teeth. The impact of this capacity-building was profound, fostering local expertise and embedding ATR deeply in the aviation cultures of diverse nations.

It is perhaps this combination of ubiquity, utility, and adaptability that earned ATR the label of a global icon. Unlike glamorous widebodies, which captured headlines with record-breaking flights or luxurious cabins, ATR aircraft did their work quietly, reliably, and everywhere. They were the unsung heroes of aviation, the machines that carried people not across oceans but across lives. Their significance was not diminished by this modesty; rather, it was magnified. For millions of passengers, ATR was aviation.

As the aviation industry pressed forward toward net-zero goals, ATR's future seemed secure. Its aircraft were poised to serve as platforms for SAF adoption and hybrid-electric innovation, ensuring continued relevance. More importantly, its mission—to connect communities—remained vital. While megacities built ever larger airports and airlines dreamed of supersonic revivals, the everyday reality of aviation was still about reaching the small places, the remote places, the overlooked places. ATR embodied that reality, and in doing so, it earned its place as a permanent fixture in aviation history.

By the time ATR celebrated its 50th anniversary in the 2030s, the contours of its achievement were clear. A company born from a pragmatic European partnership had become the world's indispensable provider of regional connectivity. Its aircraft had crossed continents and generations, bridging gaps not only of geography but of opportunity. In the quiet persistence of its turboprops lay a lesson: that aviation's greatest triumphs are not always measured in distance records or technological leaps, but in the simple, repeated act of bringing people together.

ATR's journey from a niche venture to a global icon was therefore not just the story of an aircraft manufacturer but of the role aviation plays in human society. It demonstrated that connectivity, efficiency, and resilience can define success as surely as speed or glamour. And it underscored that in the fabric of global travel, the small, steady threads of regional aviation are every bit as vital as the bold strokes of intercontinental flight.

In the end, ATR's legacy was not confined to airports or runways. It lived in the communities linked by its aircraft, in the economies strengthened by regional trade and tourism, and in the individuals whose horizons expanded because an ATR turboprop made their journey possible. That was what made ATR more than a manufacturer, and more than an aircraft. It made it a global icon of regional aviation—a symbol of flight's ability to unite the world, one short hop at a time.

Epilogue: The Enduring Balance

When aviation historians tell the story of the jet age, their narratives often soar toward the dramatic: the transatlantic crossings of the Boeing 707, the supersonic audacity of Concorde, the double-deck grandeur of the Airbus A380, or the sleek efficiency of the Boeing 787. These aircraft, with their long-haul glamour and technological daring, captured headlines and imaginations. Yet beneath the thunder of afterburners and the whisper of composite wings, another narrative persisted—quieter, humbler, but no less essential. That was the story of the turboprop, and above all, the story of ATR.

ATR's place in aviation history was not forged in the pursuit of speed records or prestige projects, but in the steady, relentless pursuit of practicality. Its aircraft flew short hops where jets would be inefficient or uneconomical, serving routes that might otherwise have been abandoned altogether. In doing so, ATR sustained the arteries of aviation's circulatory system: the small towns, remote islands, and developing markets where connectivity was a lifeline rather than a luxury. This balance—between innovation and practicality—was ATR's defining contribution.

The company's genius lay in resisting the temptation to follow the herd. At a time when the aviation industry was often obsessed with bigger, faster, and more luxurious, ATR doubled down on modesty. Its aircraft were smaller, slower, and simpler. But they were perfectly suited to the missions that most often defined daily aviation. The ATR did not compete with widebodies for the headlines of aerospace magazines; instead, it quietly accumulated flying hours, reliably delivering passengers and cargo on sectors of a few hundred miles. This was aviation stripped to its essence: the act of connecting people.

Turboprops themselves had long been overshadowed by jets, but they carried qualities that became increasingly relevant as the decades progressed. Their propeller-driven efficiency, once considered a relic of the past, emerged as a solution for a future constrained by environmental concerns. Their ability to operate from short runways and rugged airstrips offered flexibility that gleaming jets could never match. And their lower fuel burn per passenger made them indispensable in a world recalibrating its priorities toward sustainability. ATR championed these virtues not defensively, but proudly, reframing the turboprop as a tool for the future rather than a leftover of the past.

The symbolic role of ATR's aircraft lay in this reframing. They showed that progress in aviation was not only measured in leaps of speed or altitude but in refinements of purpose. ATR never stopped innovating—its avionics, cabins, and efficiency improved continually—but it innovated with discipline. The ATR 600 series was not a radical departure but a careful evolution, marrying modern cockpit technology with proven aerodynamics. The decision to pursue hybrid-electric research and sustainable aviation fuels was not a sudden pivot but a natural extension of ATR's philosophy. In every case, innovation was directed toward enhancing practicality, not chasing prestige.

This approach mirrored a deeper truth about aviation itself. The glamour of the jet age was real, but it was never the whole story. For every passenger boarding a widebody bound for New York, Tokyo, or Dubai, there were many more boarding a turboprop for the journey from one provincial city to another, from an island to the mainland, or from a rural outpost to a national capital. The global aviation ecosystem depended on these countless short flights. Without them, the network would fray, and the very notion of worldwide connectivity would falter. ATR symbolized this unseen but indispensable layer of aviation.

In cultural terms, the ATR experience was both ordinary and extraordinary. To millions of passengers across Asia, Africa, Latin America, and Europe, the sight of an ATR waiting on the apron was as familiar as the local bus. Boarding steps that unfolded onto a short fuselage, the distinctive hum of propellers spooling up, the sense of being closer to the landscape below—these details imprinted themselves into memory. While the glamour of a widebody's departure might dazzle once or twice in a lifetime, the humbler experience of an ATR became part of the fabric of everyday life. Ordinary journeys carried extraordinary significance: a student flying to university, a doctor reaching a rural clinic, a family reuniting after months apart. In these moments, the ATR was not just a machine but a conduit of human connection.

The symbolic weight of ATR's endurance was heightened by the disappearance of its competitors. One by one, Saab, Fokker, Dornier, and British Aerospace withdrew from turboprop production. Even Bombardier, with its Dash 8, eventually left the field. By the 2020s, ATR alone carried the torch. The company became not just a manufacturer but a custodian of the turboprop tradition, preserving an essential option for airlines worldwide. This uniqueness reinforced its identity as an icon. When an airline needed a modern turboprop, there was essentially one choice—and that choice carried decades of accumulated expertise.

ATR's resilience also reflected the balance between global and local. Its Franco-Italian origins tied it to Europe's industrial landscape, yet its aircraft were most often seen in skies far from Toulouse or Naples. It was, in many ways, the most global of manufacturers, with customers spread evenly across continents. That universality underscored its symbolic role: ATR was not the aircraft of one nation or one region, but of the world. Its mission transcended borders, speaking to the shared human need for mobility and connection.

As aviation moved into the age of sustainability, ATR's symbolic role only deepened. Where widebody manufacturers faced the daunting challenge of decarbonizing long-haul travel, ATR could point to immediate gains. Its aircraft already burned significantly less fuel per passenger than comparable regional jets. Compatibility with sustainable aviation fuel was a practical step, not a distant dream. And hybrid-electric propulsion, while ambitious, was most feasible in precisely the short-haul markets ATR served. In this sense, ATR embodied the balance between aspiration and reality: it represented progress grounded in the possible.

For passengers and airlines alike, this balance was a source of trust. Airlines knew that ordering ATRs was a safe bet, a choice that would yield reliable performance and manageable costs. Passengers, whether consciously or not, came to associate ATR flights with dependability and accessibility. Governments recognized ATR's importance in achieving regional development goals. Environmental advocates pointed to its efficiency as a benchmark. In every sphere, ATR represented the quiet strength of practicality.

Looking at the arc of aviation history, ATR's achievement can be seen as a counterpoint to the dominant narrative. If the jet age symbolized speed, ambition, and global reach, the ATR age symbolized endurance, adaptability, and local connection. The two narratives were not opposed but complementary. Together, they formed the full picture of modern aviation: the spectacular and the everyday, the glamorous and the grounded, the long-haul and the short-hop. ATR's place was to remind the world that aviation's greatness was not only in conquering oceans but in bridging the small gaps that mattered most to people's lives.

In the end, ATR's symbolic role was to prove that practicality itself could be visionary. By focusing on what worked, on what communities needed, and on what airlines could sustain, ATR ensured its relevance for decades. Its turboprops may never have been the fastest or the flashiest, but they were the right aircraft for their time—and, increasingly, for the times ahead. As the aviation industry faces mounting pressure to reconcile growth with sustainability, ATR's example stands as both guide and reassurance: progress need not come in giant leaps. Sometimes, it comes in steady propeller turns, carrying passengers one short flight at a time.

ATR's story, then, is not merely about airplanes. It is about the balance between ambition and realism, about the humility to serve overlooked markets, and about the vision to see value where others did not. It is about the enduring truth that aviation's power lies not only in its ability to connect continents but in its ability to connect communities. In a world that increasingly measures success in terms of sustainability, accessibility, and inclusivity, ATR emerges not just as a manufacturer of turboprops but as a symbol of aviation's best self.

As the final passengers of the day step down onto small airfields under tropical skies or alpine peaks, their ATRs cooling behind them, they may not reflect on history, innovation, or symbolism. But in their footsteps lies the living proof of ATR's legacy. Every arrival at a small airport, every bag of cargo unloaded, every connection made between people and places testifies to the enduring balance ATR struck—and to its rightful place as one of aviation's quiet, indispensable icons.

Appendix A: Chronology of ATR Aircraft Development

- **1981** – ATR (Aerei da Trasporto Regionale / Avions de Transport Régional) is formally established as a Franco-Italian joint venture between Aerospatiale (France) and Aeritalia (Italy).

- **1984** – First flight of the ATR 42 prototype takes place on August 16.

- **1985** – ATR 42 receives European certification and enters commercial service with Air Littoral of France.

- **1986** – First ATR 42 deliveries outside Europe, including operators in the Caribbean and the U.S.

- **1988** – Launch of the stretched ATR 72 program, designed to carry around 70 passengers.

- **1989** – First flight of the ATR 72 on October 27.

- **1989** – ATR 72 enters commercial service with Finnair.

- **1992** – ATR surpasses 500 aircraft delivered, cementing its place as the leading turboprop manufacturer.

- **1994** – Introduction of upgraded ATR 42-500 model, featuring new propellers and improved performance.

- **1997** – ATR 72-500 introduced with six-blade propellers and enhanced avionics.

- **1998** – ATR passes the milestone of 600 deliveries worldwide.

- **2000** – ATR celebrates its 15th anniversary in service with more than 600 aircraft operating in over 100 airlines worldwide.

- **2003** – Launch of the ATR 42-500 cargo conversion program.

- **2004** – ATR secures major fleet orders in Asia, particularly from Indian and Indonesian carriers.

- **2005** – ATR 72-500 becomes one of the most widely ordered regional aircraft in the world, with over 600 commitments.

- **2007** – ATR 600 series formally launched at the Paris Air Show, featuring a redesigned cockpit and cabin.

- **2009** – First ATR 72-600 prototype takes flight.

- **2010** – ATR 72-600 receives certification; first deliveries follow to Royal Air Maroc.

- **2011** – ATR 42-600 certified and enters service.

- **2012** – ATR achieves record annual sales, fueled by strong demand in Asia-Pacific.

- **2014** – ATR surpasses 1,000 aircraft delivered worldwide.

- **2015** – ATR introduces ATR 72-600 High Density configuration for up to 78 seats.

- **2016** – First ATR 72-600F (freighter) program announced in partnership with FedEx Express.

- **2017** – ATR delivers its 1,500th aircraft, underscoring long-term dominance of the regional turboprop market.

- **2019** – First ATR 72-600F freighter makes its maiden flight in Toulouse.

- **2020** – ATR 72-600F certified; FedEx receives the first delivery.

- **2021** – ATR introduces a "Short Take-Off and Landing" (STOL) variant of the ATR 42-600 for airports with runways under 1,000 meters.

- **2022** – ATR confirms 100% compatibility of ATR 72-600 and ATR 42-600 with Sustainable Aviation Fuel (SAF) blends up to 50%.

- **2023** – ATR 72-600 STOL moves toward entry into service, with multiple commitments from remote-region operators.

- **2024** – ATR fleet surpasses 2,000 orders in total, with more than 1,600 aircraft in active service worldwide.

This appendix gives a clear chronological flow from ATR's founding through its continuous evolution, ensuring the reader sees both the technological milestones and the scale of production.

Appendix B: Technical Specifications of Major ATR Variants

ATR 42 Family

- **ATR 42-300 (1985)**
    - First production model of the ATR family.
    - Capacity: Typically 40–50 passengers.
    - Engines: Pratt & Whitney Canada PW120 turboprops.
    - Maximum Take-Off Weight (MTOW): Approx. 16,000 kg (35,300 lb).
    - Range: About 1,500 km (930 mi).
    - Cruise Speed: 465 km/h (290 mph).
    - Notable for its role as the foundation of the ATR product line.

- **ATR 42-320 (Late 1980s)**
    - Improved engines (PW121) for hotter and higher operational environments.
    - Performance enhancements particularly suited to challenging airports in Asia and Latin America.

- **ATR 42-500 (1995)**
    - Six-bladed Hamilton Standard propellers for reduced noise and vibration.
    - Upgraded avionics and more comfortable interiors.
    - Capacity: 46–50 passengers.
    - MTOW: Around 18,600 kg (41,000 lb).
    - Range: Up to 1,500 km (930 mi).
    - Widely adopted for regional routes requiring short-field performance.
- **ATR 42-600 (2011)**
    - Modernized cockpit with glass avionics suite.
    - New interior design focused on passenger comfort.
    - Engines: PW127M turboprops.
    - Capacity: 48–50 passengers.
    - MTOW: 18,600 kg (41,000 lb).
    - Range: Approximately 1,500 km (930 mi).
    - Cruise Speed: 510 km/h (320 mph).
    - Considered the definitive version of the ATR 42 family.

- **ATR 42-600S (STOL Variant, 2020s)**

    o STOL = Short Take-Off and Landing, designed for runways as short as 800–1,000 meters.

    o Retains ATR 42-600 cabin and avionics with modified wing and rudder design.

    o Engine power increased for improved field performance.

    o Targeted for remote and island operations, especially in places like the Caribbean, French overseas territories, and mountainous regions.

ATR 72 Family

- **ATR 72-200 (1989)**

    o Stretched version of the ATR 42 to carry more passengers.

    o Capacity: 66–72 passengers.

    o Engines: PW124B turboprops.

    o MTOW: Approx. 22,500 kg (49,600 lb).

    o Range: Around 1,500 km (930 mi).

    o Entered service with Finnair.

- **ATR 72-210 (1992)**
    - Also referred to as ATR 72-210/72-210A depending on performance package.
    - Engines: PW127 engines provided higher power for hot and high environments.
    - Enhanced performance compared to ATR 72-200.
- **ATR 72-500 (1997)**
    - Six-bladed propellers reducing cabin noise and vibration.
    - Enhanced cockpit and avionics systems.
    - Capacity: 68–74 passengers.
    - MTOW: 23,000 kg (50,700 lb).
    - Range: Up to 1,500 km (930 mi).
    - Cruise Speed: 511 km/h (318 mph).
    - Became the most successful ATR variant of its generation.
- **ATR 72-600 (2010)**
    - Glass cockpit with Thales avionics suite.
    - Modernized interior with larger overhead bins and improved lighting.
    - Engines: PW127M turboprops.

- Capacity: 70–78 passengers.
- MTOW: 23,000 kg (50,700 lb).
- Range: 1,500–1,665 km (930–1,035 mi).
- Cruise Speed: 510 km/h (317 mph).
- Today's flagship model of the ATR line.

- **ATR 72-600F (Freighter, 2020)**
  - Factory-built freighter variant.
  - Payload: Up to 9 tonnes.
  - Large cargo door for containerized freight.
  - Range: Around 1,500 km (930 mi).
  - Operated initially by FedEx Express as launch customer.
  - Adapted for e-commerce and express parcel markets.

General Characteristics Across ATR Family

- **Operational Niche**: ATR aircraft are designed for short-haul flights of 200–800 km, excelling in operations from short runways and airports with limited infrastructure.

- **Performance Advantage**: Turboprops consume around 30–40% less fuel than regional jets on short routes, giving ATR aircraft an efficiency edge.

- **Global Reach**: By the 2020s, ATR aircraft are in service in more than 100 countries with over 200 operators, both passenger and cargo.

This appendix captures the **evolution of the ATR 42 and ATR 72 lines** in technical detail while emphasizing how design refinements over time sustained their global relevance.

Appendix C: Global Operator List (Past and Present)

Europe

- **Air France (France)** – Regional affiliates such as Airlinair and HOP! operated large fleets of ATR 42s and 72s, connecting smaller French cities and regional hubs.

- **Alitalia (Italy)** – Former national carrier with ATR 42s and ATR 72s used on short domestic sectors across the Italian peninsula and islands.

- **Finnair (Finland)** – Launch customer for the ATR 72, deploying it widely in Nordic operations.

- **British Airways (UK)** – Through subsidiaries such as CityFlyer Express and Brymon Airways, BA operated ATR 42s and 72s in the 1990s.

- **Aer Lingus Regional (Ireland)** – Operated by Stobart Air, ATRs formed the backbone of Aer Lingus Regional routes across Ireland and the UK.

- **Loganair (UK)** – Scotland's flag carrier has flown ATR 42s and 72s to connect remote Highlands and Islands communities.

- **Olympic Airways (Greece)** – Adopted ATRs for Greek island services.

- **Iberia Regional / Air Nostrum (Spain)** – Former operator of ATR 72s across Spain's short-haul routes.

- **LOT Polish Airlines (Poland)** – Through subsidiary EuroLOT, operated ATR 42s and 72s domestically and regionally.

- **TAP Express (Portugal)** – Operated ATR 72s through White Airways for regional feeder services.

- **CSA Czech Airlines (Czech Republic)** – Deployed ATRs extensively for short-haul European services.

- **Malmo Aviation (Sweden)** – One of several Scandinavian carriers to employ ATR turboprops.

- **Volotea (Spain)** – Early operations included ATR 72 aircraft.

- **Aurigny Air Services (Guernsey, Channel Islands)** – Lifeline operator for Channel Islands connectivity, using ATR 72s.

Asia-Pacific

- **Lion Air Group (Indonesia)** – Subsidiary Wings Air operates one of the world's largest ATR fleets, exceeding 60 ATR 72s, serving hundreds of Indonesian island routes.

- **Garuda Indonesia (Indonesia)** – Regional affiliate Citilink also flew ATRs for domestic connectivity.

- **Air India Regional / Alliance Air (India)** – Large ATR 42 and ATR 72 fleet serving smaller Indian cities.

- **IndiGo (India)** – Adopted ATR 72-600s in the late 2010s to expand connectivity to tier-two and tier-three cities.

- **SpiceJet (India)** – Operated ATR 72s on shorter domestic routes.

- **Bangkok Airways (Thailand)** – Major ATR operator across Southeast Asia, branding itself as a "boutique" regional airline.

- **Vietnam Airlines (Vietnam)** – Historically flew ATR 72s across domestic networks, particularly Hanoi–Haiphong and Ho Chi Minh–Can Tho routes.

- **Philippine Airlines (Philippines)** – Through PAL Express, operated ATR 72s connecting the Philippine islands.

- **Cebu Pacific (Philippines)** – Uses ATR 72s (operated by Cebgo) for inter-island operations, with a fleet of over 20 aircraft.

- **Malaysia Airlines (Malaysia)** – Deployed ATR 72s through its subsidiary Firefly.

- **SilkAir (Singapore)** – Regional routes formerly used ATRs before fleet standardization on jets.

- **Air Tahiti (French Polynesia)** – One of the most iconic ATR operators, connecting Polynesian islands with ATR 42s and 72s.

- **PNG Air (Papua New Guinea)** – ATRs provide lifeline services in rugged terrain and remote communities.

Africa

- **Air Mauritius (Mauritius)** – Operated ATR 72s for short flights to Réunion and Rodrigues.
- **Ethiopian Airlines (Ethiopia)** – Used ATRs in regional networks and subsidiaries.
- **Tunisair Express (Tunisia)** – Operates ATR 72s for domestic services.
- **Air Algérie (Algeria)** – Deployed ATR 42s and ATR 72s for regional connectivity.
- **ASKY Airlines (Togo)** – Operates ATRs for West African regional flights.
- **Air Burkina (Burkina Faso)** – ATR 72s are the core of its fleet.
- **Air Senegal (Senegal)** – Modern ATR 72-600s link Dakar with regional destinations.
- **Precision Air (Tanzania)** – Longtime ATR operator serving East Africa.
- **RwandAir (Rwanda)** – Operates ATR 42s and 72s on regional routes.
- **South African Express (South Africa)** – Historically flew ATR 42s.

- **TAAG Angola Airlines (Angola)** – Regional connectivity supported by ATR 72s.

- **Comair (South Africa)** – Past ATR operator in domestic services.

- **Air Namibia (Namibia)** – Brief ATR 42 operation for regional feeder services.

Latin America and the Caribbean

- **Avianca (Colombia)** – Deployed ATR 72-600s across domestic and regional routes.

- **LATAM Airlines Group (Chile/Brazil/Peru)** – Various regional affiliates used ATR 42s and 72s.

- **TAME (Ecuador)** – ATRs flew in mountainous terrain to connect Andean cities.

- **Conviasa (Venezuela)** – ATRs provided essential connectivity.

- **Caribbean Airlines (Trinidad & Tobago)** – ATR 72s operated on inter-island services.

- **LIAT (Antigua & Barbuda)** – One of the most famous Caribbean ATR operators, with a fleet of ATR 42s and 72s connecting islands.

- **Cayman Airways (Cayman Islands)** – ATR 72s form a core part of its fleet.

- **Bahamasair (Bahamas)** – ATR 42s and 72s support extensive island-hopping routes.

- **Cubana de Aviación (Cuba)** – Operated ATR 42s and 72s.
- **Aeromar (Mexico)** – A long-standing operator with ATR 42s and 72s.
- **SATENA (Colombia)** – Military-run regional carrier using ATRs in remote Colombia.

Middle East

- **Iran Air (Iran)** – Operated ATR 72s domestically.
- **Mahan Air (Iran)** – ATRs used for secondary city routes.
- **SyrianAir (Syria)** – Historic ATR operator.
- **Oman Air (Oman)** – ATR 42s used for short routes inside Oman and to nearby Gulf countries.
- **Royal Jordanian (Jordan)** – Deployed ATRs through Royal Wings for regional flights.
- **Kuwait Airways (Kuwait)** – Brief ATR 72 operator.

North America

- **American Eagle (United States)** – Several regional partners operated ATR 42s and 72s in the 1990s and 2000s, including Simmons Airlines and Executive Airlines in Puerto Rico.
- **Continental Connection (United States)** – Gulfstream International Airlines flew ATR 42s and 72s.

- **Delta Connection (United States)** – Subsidiaries such as Comair and ASA flew ATR 72s in the 1990s.

- **US Airways Express (United States)** – Carriers such as Simmons Airlines operated ATR 42s.

- **Air Canada Jazz (Canada)** – Operated ATR 42s and 72s before fleet consolidation.

- **Calm Air (Canada)** – Major operator in Manitoba with ATR 42s and 72s, including combi aircraft.

- **First Air (Canada)** – ATR 42s with gravel kits served Arctic and northern communities.

- **Canadian North (Canada)** – Continues to operate ATR 42s in northern conditions.

Notes on Fleet Distribution

- **Largest Fleets**: Wings Air (Indonesia), IndiGo (India), Alliance Air (India), and Lion Air affiliates maintain the largest ATR fleets, often 50–70+ aircraft.

- **Longest Operators**: Airlines such as Air Tahiti, Aeromar (Mexico), and LIAT in the Caribbean have been almost synonymous with ATR for decades.

- **Cargo Operators**: In addition to passenger carriers, FedEx Express, Swiftair (Spain), and ASL Airlines (Europe) operate ATR freighters.

- **Diversity of Users**: From tiny island carriers with one or two aircraft to multinational groups with dozens, ATR's operator base is among the widest of any aircraft manufacturer.

www.ingramcontent.com/pod-product-compliance
Ingram Content Group UK Ltd.
Pitfield, Milton Keynes, MK11 3LW, UK
UKHW020710220925
8009UKWH00042B/614